The Outwin Boochever

PORTRAIT
COMPETITION
2013

The Outwin Boochever
PORTRAIT COMPETITION 2013

Foreword
Wendy Wick Reaves

Essay
Mary Sheriff

About the Artists
Dorothy Moss

Smithsonian
National Portrait Gallery
Washington, D.C.

Published to accompany the
Outwin Boochever Portrait Competition
March 23, 2013–February 23, 2014
National Portrait Gallery, Smithsonian Institution

ISBN: 978-0-9786657-3-9

Library of Congress Control Number: 2012955902

Editorial and production management:
Dru Dowdy, Head of Publications, National Portrait Gallery

Design: Debra Naylor, Naylor Design, Inc., Washington, D.C.

Printing: Four Colour Print Group, Louisville, Kentucky

CONTENTS

FOREWORD

Wendy Wick Reaves, Interim Director,
National Portrait Gallery

After a long career at the National Portrait Gallery, I have spent my professional life looking at and thinking about portraiture. One might think I had seen it all. One also might guess I had a pretty firm internal definition of what constitutes a good likeness, a realistic expression of personality, and a definitive measure of character. Happily, as the Outwin Boochever Portrait Competition illustrates, one would guess wrong on all those points. Likeness, personality, and character are intangible assets that elude rigid visual interpretation. Innovative portraitists may focus on one or another of them or manage to capture an individual effectively without reference to any of the three.

The Outwin Boochever Portrait Competition repeatedly proves the point. The 2013 competition exhibition, our third in just over six years, provides the same exhilarating moments of surprise as its predecessors. These exhibitions vibrate with fresh ideas, challenging approaches, and, generally, a slight frisson of controversy. Viewers will inevitably disagree about the choice of artworks, the lack of consistency, and the selection of prize-winners, but few leave without a revelation of one kind or another. Whatever fixed ideas about portraiture a visitor brings is likely to be challenged.

Many of our jurors commented on the variety of style, medium, approach, and subject matter in this exhibition. Is there any commonality amidst all this glorious diversity? I think perhaps there is. In reviewing the final selection one more time, I repeatedly sensed a quality that I might call authenticity. So many of our choices conveyed a thoughtful and deeply felt interaction with the individual represented (self or other), a respect for medium, a dedication to craft, and creative imagination. Perhaps Hung Liu references a similar idea when she advises her students that "you have to create something you really believe in." These life portraits communicate the artists' real, authentic experiences in a compelling way. Heart and soul claim a place in this exhibition.

The late Virginia Outwin Boochever, who served as a docent at the National Portrait Gallery for many years, shared her passion for portraiture with visitors. Her generosity subsequently launched the first truly national portrait competition in this country in 2006, a legacy that continues today. Mrs. Boochever's enthusiasm for portraiture is echoed by the 3,300 entries from all over the country, the diversity of our artists and their submissions, and the excitement of our panel of jurors. This generous donor and the portrait competition that she began continually reinforce the enduring appeal of that malleable art of portraying identity. We welcome portraiture's provocation and its mutability, which ensures that it will intrigue innovative artists long into the future.

VIRGINIA OUTWIN BOOCHEVER

An Appreciation

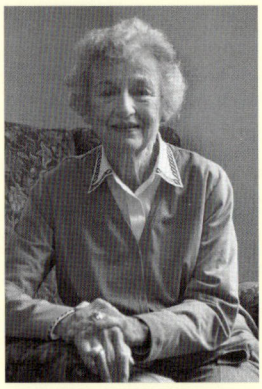

Virginia Outwin Boochever
by Jim Gipe, 2001. National
Portrait Gallery, Smithsonian
Institution; gift of Virginia
Boochever, courtesy of
Smith College

Virginia Outwin Boochever (1920–2005) was born in Newark, New Jersey, and grew up in nearby Maplewood, where her father was the president of a medical supply company. After graduating from Smith College in 1941, she became one of the first female commissioned officers in the Navy WAVES. In 1945, she married Louis C. Boochever Jr., a U.S. Foreign Service officer, and for the next thirty years dedicated herself to raising four children and to the diplomatic life that took the family to Luxembourg, Paris, Belgrade, Rome, and Brussels. Gregarious and curious, she took pleasure in learning about the art and culture of the countries where she lived and engaging the myriad people she met.

In 1974, the Boochevers moved to Washington, D.C., where Mrs. Boochever took on a variety of volunteer activities. She was most passionate, however, about her work as a docent at the National Portrait Gallery. Appreciation of art was a lifelong interest: as a young woman she had studied art at the graduate level, and she and her husband were enthusiastic collectors. For nearly two decades, Mrs. Boochever delighted Portrait Gallery visitors with her knowledge of the artworks, especially of the subjects' lives and times. She moved to Brunswick, Maine, in 2003.

Always interested in people, Mrs. Boochever saw the endowment of a portrait competition at the National Portrait Gallery as a way to benefit artists directly. Her knowledge of the portrait museums of England and Australia allowed her to understand the role that their competitions play in encouraging portraiture, and she saw the endowment as a unique opportunity to fill a void in the American art world.

THE PORTRAIT NOW AND THEN

Mary Sheriff

What makes a portrayal a portrait? Do we rely on the experts—the artists, historians, and critics—to answer this question for us? Or in seeking commonly held belief, do we consult the dictionary, the encyclopedia, or an art history textbook? Or do we with some embarrassment rush to our computers and call up Wikipedia? It was there that I found a useful definition of "portrait" as it is widely conceived today: "A portrait is a painting, photograph, sculpture, or other artistic representation of a person, in which the face and its expression is predominant. The intent is to display the likeness, personality, and even the mood of the person." I like the simplicity of this definition, which, although contemporary, points to the essential qualities that historically belonged to portraiture as a genre. Yet as simple as the Wikipedia definition may be, it also calls for reflection in positing that a portrait is an artistic representation made with the specific intention to display something. And primary among those qualities the portrait artist intends to display is likeness.

The question of intention seems important in considering the finalists in the Outwin Boochever Portrait Competition. Can we discern what each artist intended to put on display? Given that their works are entries into a competition, each likely chose a piece that best demonstrated the ability to make an "artistic representation of a person." But did they also select one that highlighted likeness to a specific individual? If we judged solely from entries' titles, we might have our doubts. Although works called *Leslie* and *Kevin* seem to announce this intention, others, such as *Red Robe* or *Life Raft*, do not. Perhaps some artists presumed that likeness was not an issue in the competition since only those who know or who have at least seen the individual portrayed can presume to judge resemblance. Yet titles such as *Life Raft* point away from portraiture.

At least since the advent of national art academies in the seventeenth century, portraiture stood at a rank below that of subjects drawn from history, religion, or the allegorical tradition, for these required artists to imagine what they had never seen and compose narratives with complex figural groups. Portraiture was presumed to demand only a simple imitation of nature, even if it required considerable skill at producing artistic effects. Throughout history, portraitists elevated their genre by placing portraits within other recognizable categories. They presented the sitter in allegorical disguise as a god or goddess, or they embedded the portrait in a larger narrative. Although today we have abandoned the traditional hierarchy of genres, many competition entries embellish the portrait by framing it with a story, presenting it as allegory, or in some way asking viewers to do more than recognize the sitter.

Consider, for example, Katie O'Hagan's *Life Raft* (fig. 1). At the center of the painting we see a young woman crouched on a small raft, adrift from any visible shore. Although the steel-blue sea is relatively calm, the sky is cloud-filled and the woman's look apprehensive. Indeed, both her hair and chemise are disheveled, as if she has narrowly escaped some unseen disaster. But her pose and expression have multiple connotations. With her head turned slightly away from her body and her eyes cast upward, she could be judging an oncoming storm, seeking divine aid, or searching for inspiration. Her pose alludes, if only inadvertently, to a long tradition of artists who, in taking their cue from the evangelists, implored heaven to guide their hands. These possibilities are keyed to what this castaway is actually doing: painting—or better said, creating—a life raft. Brush in hand, she applies more dark-grey pigment to complete her task. The action suggests that this work is a self-portrait, and its portrait-like qualities are represented in the woman's individualized features. In fact, this work is a good likeness of Katie O'Hagan if we can judge from the photograph on her website. Yet the work interests us as much in its clever play with artifice—a ruse that has characterized self-portraits throughout history—as in its quality of likeness.

If O'Hagan's pose suggests the inspiration that has guided her hand, what has inspired her is not the heavens but the history of art. Her work might be construed as a postmodern riff on Théodore Géricault's *The Raft of the Medusa* (fig. 2), raising the

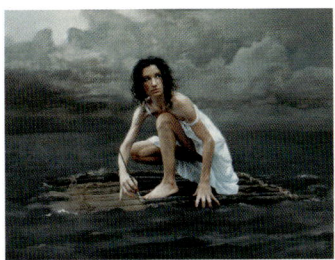

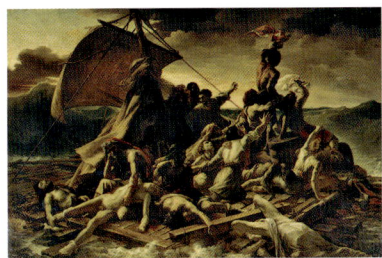

Fig. 1. *Life Raft* by Katie O'Hagan. See page 63

Fig. 2. *The Raft of the Medusa* by Théodore Géricault (1791–1824), oil on canvas, 1819. Musée du Louvre, Paris, France

portrait to the level of narrative. Yet in some sense every work of art also represents a particular "hand," mind, sensibility, or manner. In the nineteenth century, French critics emphasized that a good portrayal was a "portrait of" at least two individuals: the person portrayed and the artist who made the portrayal. Their claim articulated what had been the norm for centuries: an excellent portrait displayed both likeness and artistic skill. This proposition seems obvious, but achieving the right balance in a portrait could be challenging.

The expectation that artists would adhere to prevailing canons of resemblance posed the obvious question of how the artist's artistry was best displayed and made to serve likeness. Was it most evident when art hid art, i.e., when artists showed superior talent by hiding the marks of a particular style or effacing evidence of their intervention? In that case artists displayed themselves paradoxically by remaining invisible. Or was the portrait most valued when it showcased the personal manner of a celebrated virtuoso but offered less resemblance? There the significant likeness would lie between the status of the artist and that of the patron who could command the services of a master. Thus while portraiture long held "likeness" as a norm, likeness to what remained a fundamental question.

At some historical moments "likeness" was dependent on portraying individual traits with exactitude; at other times idealized portraits became the standard. Sometimes likeness was construed as adherence to an established convention (as in the case of portraits of rulers) or to current modes of dress or adornment. And "likeness" could be rendered in relation to invisible qualities, such as personality, status, or taste. At each historical moment, moreover, several modes of likeness were available, and the artist was expected to consider variables such as the sitter's social standing, the location for which the work was intended, and of course the patron's desires. Notions of "art" also influenced portrait-making. It is only recently that a portrait could be rendered as an installation, such as Saeri Kiritani's *100 Pounds of Rice* (p. 59). There the artist creates likeness by making a portrait of herself as an Asian American in a nontraditional material—rice—that although widely consumed throughout the world is nevertheless associated with Asian culture. In presenting the artist and her image as constituted from the same material in the same quantity, the installation self-consciously parodies the stereotype that renders all Asians alike. Often placed in the back of the installation, a representation of Kiritani's *Rice Myself* (fig. 3) intensifies the correspondence between real and sculpted bodies and repeats the mimicry that renders the stereotype absurd: in that work Kiritani covered her body with a second skin of rice and donned a wig of rice noodles.

Although only a few of the portraits in this competition work with untraditional materials and forms, all wrestle with two perennial questions: how to balance resemblance and artistry, and how to make a portrait that exceeds its generic definition as the "artistic rendering of an individual." David Kassan takes on both challenges in *Portrait of My Mom, Roberta* (fig. 4). In some ways the painting appears to erase the intervention of the artist

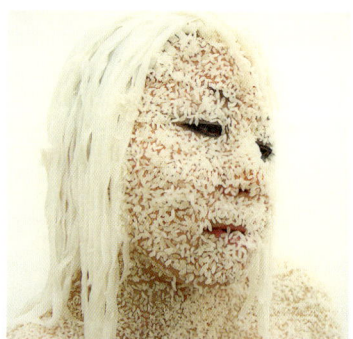

Fig. 3. *Rice Myself* by Saeri Kiritani, digital photograph on acrylic mount, 2011. Collection of the artist

and promote direct confrontation with the sitter. The particularized features and detailing of wrinkles, veins, and sagging flesh suggest an individualized likeness, and the sitter appears to meet us eye-to-eye as she looks out of the frame. Kassan furthers this sense of direct confrontation by erasing the marks of his brush, at least in representing Roberta. At the same time, the work draws attention to itself as art in

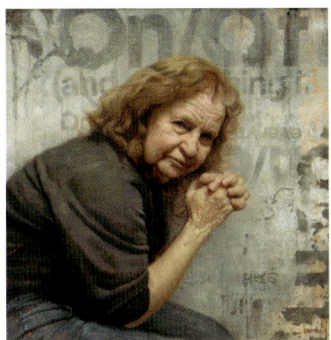

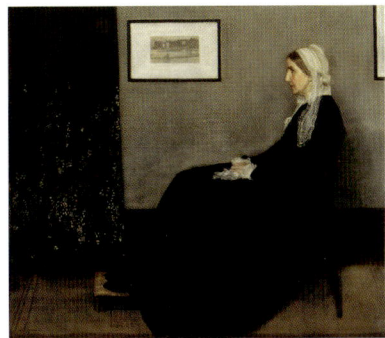

Fig. 4. *Portrait of My Mom, Roberta* by David Kassan. See page 58

Fig. 5. *Arrangement in Grey and Black No. 1, also called Portrait of the Artist's Mother* by James Abbott McNeill Whistler (1834–1903), oil on canvas, 1871. Musée d'Orsay, Paris, France

the painterly background filled with undecipherable marks and letters. Thus in placing a painted figure that seems transparent to the real against an opaque, painterly background, the portrait claims to be both nature itself and entirely artifice. The work, in fact, proposes no chance encounter with the mother, who is carefully and artfully posed. And although Roberta is hunched over with hands firmly clasped in a prayerlike gesture, when combined with her focused gaze, her posture does not suggest resigned acceptance of declining strength.

Although artists from Albrecht Dürer to Salvador Dalí portrayed their mothers, today the best known maternal portrait is Whistler's depiction of his mother, entitled *Arrangement in Grey and Black #1* (fig. 5). Here is a good example of a work that both in title and appearance draws attention to the portrait as an artful composition of colors arranged on the canvas. Kassan's portrait might be called *Arrangement in Grey and Darker Grey*, for it is rendered in a subtle palette enlivened primarily by the auburn of Roberta's hair. Yet whereas Whistler transformed his mother into an aesthetic object drained of personhood, Roberta appears as a living subject staring at us with an appraising eye. Kassan's portrait therefore recalls both the psychic power of the mother and the objectifying power of the gaze, here turned on the real viewer.

Seeing and Being Seen

The representation of the gaze—of the sitter's look—has long been central to portraiture, its potential for an uncanny effect summarized in the idea that the sitter's eyes can appear to follow the viewer from place to place. Sometimes the artist sidesteps this potential and diverts the sitter's gaze from the viewer. We find this approach in two photographic portraits that otherwise differ from one another: Veronika Adaskova's *Elisabeth* (p. 37) and Caitlin Price's *Leslie* (p. 67). Elisabeth is seated in what we take as her kitchen with her attention directed across the picture plane. The stretch of her arm as well as her gaze point us to the part of the room hidden from view: she might be observing something on that side of the room or conversing with someone outside the frame. Whatever the case, Elisabeth appears at ease in familiar surroundings, attentive but relaxed and without a hint of strong emotion visible on her face. Here, photography emphasizes neither the artist's intervention nor the confrontation with a sitter's gaze. In its apparently transparent representation of Elisabeth and her surroundings, it delivers visual pleasure through rich details and saturated colors. Leslie, in contrast, appears lost in her thoughts as she stands seemingly out of place in some uncertain terrain marked by a highway overpass—a no-place that could be anywhere. In its studied composition and arbitrary lighting, the portrait suggests not only the intervention of the photographer but also that of the close-up film still whose look it imitates. But what interests me about Price's photograph is the intense illumination of Leslie's features, and how Price draws attention to the eyes. The blue coat reprises the eye color and the shape of the earrings, that of the ocular orbs. And echoing the eyes in both shape and color are the coat's round blue buttons, which like the earrings operate as *ocelli*, the eyelike spots that provide camouflage for fish, butterflies, and other creatures. Yet rather than confuse the predator, these *ocelli* bring our notice to Leslie's real eyes and make evident that in her distracted gaze she does not attend to her surroundings. Although keeping her thoughts to herself, Leslie becomes vulnerable to the voyeurism of others who are free to devour her image.

The eyes take a very different turn in Anne Harris's self-portrayal *Red Robe* (fig. 6), which represents the artist's gaze not only as a particular way of conceiving a subject but also as a way of preying on the external world. Looking casually at this

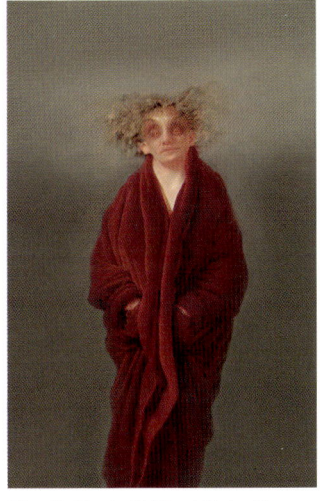

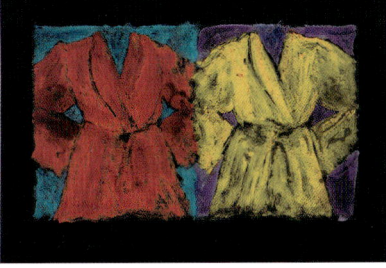

Fig. 7. *The Henry Street Robes* by Jim Dine (born 1935), black and white spitbite etching with Epson color inks, 2006. Kalamazoo Institute of Arts, Michigan; Elisabeth Claire Lahti Fund Purchase

Fig. 6. *Portrait (Red Robe)* by Anne Harris. See page 55

work, we see a woman who has just climbed out of bed, not yet fully awake. In this context, the eponymous robe is the work's subject, signifying as an ordinary, if somewhat luxurious, cover-up. Yet the robe also reveals Harris's connection to a tradition of artists portrayed in their *robes de chambre*, from Pierre Mignard to Jim Dine (fig. 7), while the stylized manner and anatomical distortions invoke her own work. With artists such as Egon Schiele, Harris repeatedly subjects her image and those of others to distortion for expressive effect. Yet what, exactly, does *Red Robe* express? A disheveled woman in a bathrobe suggests the vulnerability of first awakening, when the mind is not clear and the body not tidied up. The red robe grabs attention, but in covering her body and hands, it also allows head and face to stand out. Harris lavishes attention on the eyes, which seem to be both slightly opened and gaping wide: the first effect created by the drooping lids, the second by color washes that encircle the eyes and brows set unnaturally high. Also demanding attention are the serpentine locks transformed into electrified energy that leaves its shadow on the ground against which the figure is placed. That ground is further activated by both broadly brushed, irregular areas of pigment and shadowing whose nervous outline repeats the lines that define the ripples of the oversized robe. As the artist stares out from within this force

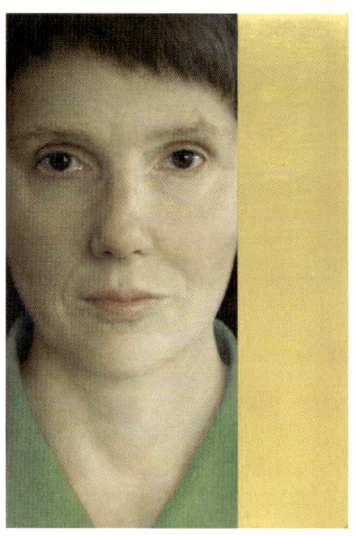

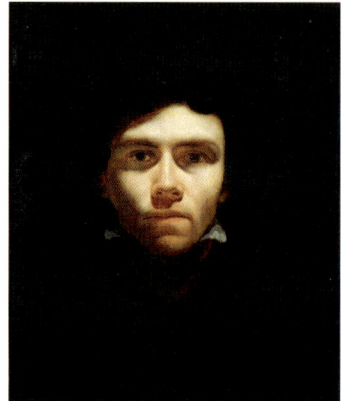

Fig. 9. *Self-Portrait* by Eugène Delacroix (1798–1863), oil on canvas, about 1816. Musée des Beaux Arts, Rouen, France

Fig. 8. *The Birth of Inez Imake* by Ginny Stanford. See page 72

field, her unruly hair and emphatic eyes lend her gaze something of Medusa's power. Indeed, all portrait-makers in a sense share in the power of the gorgon, whose gaze transforms an animated being into a representation of itself.

In a very different mode, the artist's gaze becomes powerful in Ginny Stanford's self-portrait, *The Birth of Inez Imake* (fig. 8). The title suggests a play with an alter ego, and the term "Imake" belongs to the digital age in contradictory ways. Some websites use "Imake" to signal that unique, hand-crafted objects are available for purchase, yet "Imake" also names a computer program used to generate files from a template and improve software portability from system to system. Stanford's title indicates that the person being born is alternately a maker of unique creations and a creator of repeatable templates. In portraying herself, the artist both copies her physical appearance by hand and transports to this work her technique of framing the sitter with strips of gold leaf. Yet here the gold, applied only on one side, defines the edge of a narrow opening through which the artist—a voyeur at her peephole—appears to stare. In that aperture, the artist presents herself full-face frontal, with wide eyes, immobile features, and a neutral expression. The features seem somewhat individualized, but the overall rendering of the face is generalized without

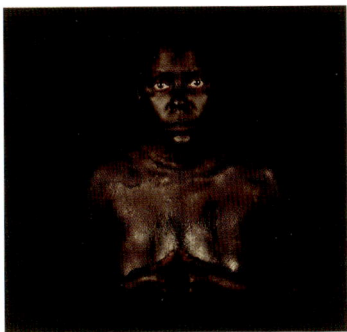

Fig. 10. *For Delia* by Heidi Fancher.
See page 32

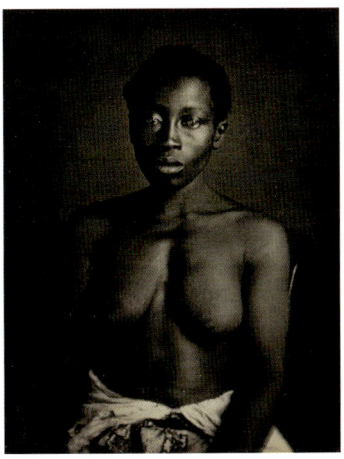

Fig. 11. *Delia* by Joseph T. Zealy (1812–1893), daguerreotype, March 1850. Peabody Museum of Archaeology and Ethnology, Harvard University, 35-5-10/ 53040 / Digital file #60742034

attending to every imperfection, and the traits show balance and symmetry. Her self-presentation thus recalls and remakes a tradition that has represented the artist's powerful vision in a similar format since the Romantic period. Like Eugène Delacroix's early self-portrait portrayals (fig. 9), the artist borrowed this representation of power from images of the emperor, such as those of Otto III or Napoleon I. In this transfer of power, the pose took on new significance pointing not to the God-given right to rule but to the artist's creative insight. Stanford personalizes this tradition, eschewing nineteenth-century romanticism but posing as an artist-voyeur who gains power through her observations of others.

Dramatically different from Stanford's full-face frontal self-portrait is Heidi Fancher's *For Delia* (fig. 10), in which the black figure is presented as both seer and apparition. The work responds to the photograph of a slave woman (fig. 11) taken in 1850 for naturalist Louis Agassiz, who sought to demonstrate the supposed biological inferiority of black Africans. Fancher's work is dedicated to the slave called Delia, and it brilliantly rebuts Agassiz's racist science in a photograph that exploits the chromographic print process for its ability to produce intense, varied blacks and whites. Fancher's figure appears to emerge before our eyes: the face and upper body have already separated from the darker ground, while the hair and elbows are not yet in full view. Our attention is drawn to the eyes, black orbs set off by spots of reflected light and brilliant white surrounds. The stare directs the energies outward and suggests this apparition's visionary gaze, yet the position of the arms and hands retracts the energy inward, rendering the figure self-contained, even protective of some vulnerability—or perhaps of some secret contained within. The striations on the chest suggest that the body has been marked or scarred. Are these ritual scarifications that designate the figure as a seer, or are they remnants of abuse, the heritage of enslavement? Whatever interpretation we give them, they are combined with light reflected at precisely the point where the thumbs ask us to look: at the figure's metaphoric heart. So represented, the thumbs also point toward some interior state, while the placement of the hands approaches, but does not reach, that of prayer. The image, moreover, veers toward androgyny, which, when combined with the apparition-like presentation, reminds us that androgyny was long associated with different forms of the occult and the mystical. There is a calculated sense of otherworldliness about this portrait in which blackness is not only a skin color but also, and more significantly, a space and a medium in which beauty and spirit can emerge.

The Portrait Then and Now

If I have focused on how portraits implicitly invoke the past, it is because the past of art, as contemporary painter Gerhard Richter shows, cannot be escaped. Many of the portrait competition's finalists obliquely, and even inadvertently, refer to the past, either through grappling with the perennial issues of portrait-making or invoking longstanding conventions. Yet two artists take on the past quite directly. In *Sensazione: A Self-Portrait* (p. 36), Leslie Adams positions herself between the past and present, drawing on the longstanding convention of showing oneself at the easel surrounded by symbolic objects. The portrait of Leonardo da Vinci on the table beside her directs our attention backwards, while her nearby glasses and the MRI brain scans posted behind bring us forward to our own age. Together these objects illuminate the title of the work, *Sensazione*, which refers to one of Leonardo's principles—specifically that of responding to sensation, as outlined in Michael Gelb's *How to Think Like Leonardo Da Vinci*. Adams raises self-portraiture to allegory and manifesto, claiming a relation between art and science as intellectual, image-making activities that engage senses, brains, and hands.

The engagement with the past at first seems to be the primary feature of Keliy Anderson-Staley's *Kevin* (p. 38). The image was produced through the outdated technology of the wet-plate collodion tintype, and unlike other recent tintypes, it does not proclaim its contemporaneity through costume or activity. We also see in *Kevin* a subtle interplay that separates what is past from what is present while allowing both to coexist in a single frame. Thus, for example, if the past is also suggested through the cut corners that mimic the current look of earlier tintypes, the image size points elsewhere. Historic tintypes were small, with full plates of 6½ x 8½ inches. Here the scale (46 x 36 inches) suggests considerable enlarging, which was not possible in the original processes. Because we often depend on fashion to judge the time frame, *Kevin*'s simple white shirt might at first leave us wondering when the image was taken, yet that garment also belies the references to earlier times. Tintypes from the past present well-dressed sitters posed for the camera; preserving likeness seems to be the primary objective. In *Kevin*, emphasis on the architecture of body and face suggests an approach that is overtly artful. Kevin's pose and averted gaze intensify in a seemingly deliberate way the "dreamy, dark, and remarkably detailed" presentation possible in the tintype.[1] Anderson-Staley thus creates a subtle work that refers to the remaking of the past in the present with a minimum of iconographical details and a maximum of historical knowledge.

It is only by looking at images that we understand the complexity of portrait-making. If by definition a portrait is "an artistic representation of a person," in practice it is more, and much more than I have suggested here. A portrait is the depiction of relations among people and within society, as in Edgar Jerins's *David and Anita Visiting Daina* (p. 57). It is an image of aspirations in Sean Cheetham's *Champagne Wishes and Caviar Dreams . . .* (p. 42) and the evocation of labor in Willard Dixon's *Mike* (p. 46). Jason Hanasik shows us the portrait as social critique in *Sharrod (Turn/Twirl)* (p. 53), and Carolyn Schlam gives dignity to old age in *Frances at 103* (p. 68). And the portrait is, and will continue to be, the way we remember our loved ones, see ourselves as we once were, and preserve our national histories.

1. Andy Wright and Reyhan Harmanci, "A Haunting Old Photographic Process Reappears," *Bay Citizen,* September 2, 2011; reprinted in the *New York Times* online edition, http://www.nytimes.com/2011/09/02/us/02bcculture. html?_r=2&src=tp&smid=fb-share&

The Outwin Boochever
PORTRAIT COMPETITION 2013

The National Portrait Gallery's third installation of its triennial portrait competition highlights the excellence and innovation of today's portraits by focusing on the variety of artistic media used by contemporary artists. This competition encourages emerging and midcareer artists to explore the ever-evolving art of portraiture. Artists over the age of eighteen who were living and working within the United States were eligible to enter from September 1 through October 31, 2012.

The Jurors

Brandon Brame Fortune, *chief curator, National Portrait Gallery, Washington, D.C.*

Peter Frank, *writer, curator, and critic, Los Angeles, California*

Hung Liu, *artist and professor, Mills College, Oakland, California*

Dorothy Moss, *assistant curator of painting and sculpture, National Portrait Gallery, Washington, D.C.*

Richard J. Powell, *John Spencer Bassett Professor of Art & Art History and professor of African/ African American studies, Duke University, Durham, North Carolina*

Wendy Wick Reaves, *interim director, National Portrait Gallery, Washington, D.C.*

Alec Soth, *artist, Minneapolis, Minnesota*

The Prize Winners

First Prize

Bo Gehring
$25,000 prize, plus a commission to create a portrait of a well-known living American for the National Portrait Gallery's collection

Second Prize
Jennifer Levonian, $7,500

Third Prize
Sequoyah Aono, $5,000

Commended Artists
Paul D'Amato, $1,000
Martha Mayer Erlebacher, $1,000
Heidi Fancher, $1,000
Beverly McIver, $1,000

JURORS' COMMENTS

Portraits are so incredibly varied. One of the strengths of the Outwin Boochever Portrait Competition is, I think, that it recognizes the value of both innovation and tradition. I love that there are some very beautifully painted portraits in oil on canvas that will be on view next to innovative conceptual works in fiber, or even portraits made of rice or thread. With the investigation and exploration of humanity as the through line, the portrait competition shows us the richness of that project. It was a pleasure to see that all of the jurors recognized this and embraced such a variety of work.

Brandon Brame Fortune

The "luck of the draw" determines any juried exhibition, and we have reason to be pleased with this year's draw. We attracted a very diverse but sophisticated and intelligent range of submissions, precisely what we'd hoped for—and required. This selection is, to my mind, where American portraiture is. It certainly looks like America (if I may trot out the cliché). And it looks like America not simply in the complexion, literally and figuratively, of the subject matter, but in the range of styles and sensibilities that have manifested in our selection and, behind that, in the self-selection of all those who entered the competition. I think the variety embodied in our necessarily limited selection reflects the variety of submissions overall, but it also reflects the variety of artistic activity in America and the range of expression possible here. We have always been a multicultural society, practically founded on a principle of creative miscegenation. This exhibition, I believe, displays that principle—not because we wanted it to, but because it wants to.

Peter Frank

Portraiture is not a fixed idiom, like a realistic rendering of a person's facial features. It's a composite of all the ways we can think of picturing ourselves and each other. This competition represents a diversity of subjects and approaches to portraiture. I, for one, work from historical Chinese photographs, but the blurrier the photograph the better—I like to fill in what's missing with what I can summon as a painter, like the missing color and materiality of the ghosts whose images haunt the faces of history. Portrayal is a lot more than the imitation of appearances. There are a lot of stories behind the picture.

Hung Liu

Reviewing more than three thousand entries to the competition was moving. I started by looking closely at the images but then would often become absorbed in the stories behind the portraits, as told in the artists' statements. When the portrait told the story before I read it—when I *heard* the artist's voice clearly in the work—I knew the portrait was successful. In those mesmerizing moments when the intimate dynamic between subject and artist emerges, even in the smallest detail, something profound happens for the viewer. When the jurors came together for the final meeting, we knew when a portrait worked in this way, and there really wasn't a lot of debate. For me, it was magic to see the panel of highly opinionated jurors in complete agreement. This is how the prizewinners were chosen.

Dorothy Moss

I am really interested in how artists can look at other people or themselves and come up with interesting, telling, and provocative ways of representing the self; sometimes in a representational way, sometimes in a more abstract way, and sometimes in ways that may characterize an inner reality. I find all of those methods very intriguing.

One of my favorite portraits is a work that got honorable mention: Beverly McIver's *Depression*. It's an image that describes how she felt about the challenges facing her after the death of her mother. But even if I didn't know that story, I would still be able to pick up on what the artwork means; with the head to one side, it's literally like an object has fallen to the floor. You really feel the visceralness of those emotions, and that's what you want in a portrait.

Richard J. Powell

As I walked around with my fellow jurors reviewing semifinalists' works, I realized we had assembled a very talented and experienced set of eyeballs. We started talking about our reactions, finishing each others' sentences as we homed in on why we experienced each work as we did. We didn't always agree. But more often than not, there was a wonderful convergence of opinion.

The vitality and diversity of the artwork excited all of us. We were delighted with the imaginative video submissions, charmed by some unusual media, struck by the raw honesty of some pictures, seduced by the mystery of others. Startling innovation shared space with echoes of past traditions. The diversity of subjects matched the variety of technique, mood, size, and media. But the absence of any distinct themes suggested to me that portraiture is in a healthy place right now, embraced by artists in different ways all over the country.

Wendy Wick Reaves

I often say I have a "no-jury" clause in my contract. I don't want to be that guy. I don't want to be *the juror*. But I've had an exhibition with the National Portrait Gallery and feel an affection for the organization. I also like that the Outwin Boochever Portrait Competition is interdisciplinary. Since I wasn't locked into my medium and it wasn't just a local competition, I felt good about it and excited to do it. One thing that was really notable about this whole process was how strong the video was, and that was unexpected. It was so fresh and so alive. In particular, the winner of the competition prize was a striking work both technically and as a portrait. The one thing I'd like to say about the selected video work is that it functions so well as portraiture—showing another human being and giving information, insight, and feeling about his or her life.

Alec Soth

Jessica Wickham
by Bo Gehring

Bo Gehring's background in mathematics, engineering, and computer graphics is revealed in his technically sophisticated sculptures and video portraits. *Jessica Wickham* is part of a concept that grew out of several years of making sculptures of music wave forms translated into complex surfaces and realized on a CNC milling machine. Gehring sees his video portraits as "linear descendants of the first photographic portraits" but with the added "richness of time and motion to help bring the subject to life." He is particularly intrigued by the mid-nineteenth-century notion that a photograph might capture a person's spirit; his portraits connect to this idea through the investigation of his subjects' emotional response to music.

Gehring's process begins with asking his subject to choose a favorite piece of music to listen to while reclining on the cloth-covered platform of an industrial milling machine. He then attaches a video camera to the machine, which scans the entire body while the music is played. The camera is tightly controlled and timed to synchronize with the length of the piece of music. Textures of clothes and skin are meticulously revealed as the machine allows the camera access to the subject at a distance closer than the human eye can focus. As Gehring explains, "Minute actions like breathing and pulse are living, vibrant elements" of the portrait and create an image that poignantly "captures emotional response over time."

Jessica Wickham is one of several portraits of people who live and work around Beacon, New York, where Gehring's studio is located. A precision woodworker (with a former banking career in Japan), Wickham makes a living creating beautifully designed furniture. Gehring portrays her in worn and soiled work clothes absorbed in the transcendent sounds of Estonian composer Arvo Pärt's "Cantus in Memoriam Benjamin Britten."

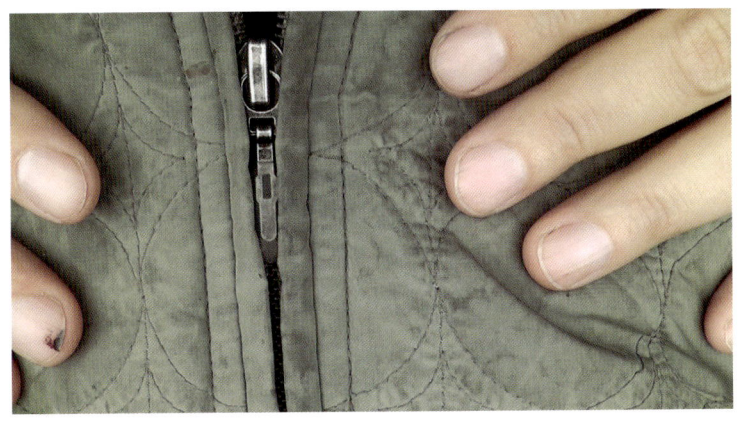

Jessica Wickham
By Bo Gehring, Beacon, New York

HD video, 5:05 minutes, 2010
Collection of the artist

Buffalo Milk Yogurt
by Jennifer Levonian

Jennifer Levonian's career took a surprising turn from figurative painting to watercolor animation when she enrolled in a course in cut-paper animation as a graduate student at the Rhode Island School of Design. She describes this experience as "an unexpected but fluid transition." The humorous, whimsical character of her work belies the time-intensive process. Levonian's stunning, detailed scenes emerge from a method that can take up to three or four months of continuous work to create one short animated video portrait. She begins with direct interaction with her subjects, taking photographs of them as source material. As Levonian explains, watercolor is her medium of choice, in part because it dries quickly, which helps move the process along.

In *Buffalo Milk Yogurt*, Levonian portrays her friend Corey Fogal having a breakdown in a Bread and Circus grocery store. The inspiration for this offbeat narrative derives from an undergraduate sociology assignment in which students were asked to stand for an extended period of time in the middle of a grocery store and observe the social codes that dominate the public spaces of a food market, such as the cheese display or the cereal aisle. When Levonian met musician Fogal for the first time at an arts conference in Florida, he was experiencing a creative block. She asked him if he would be willing to be the subject of a portrait that explored this state of mind while also referencing the sociology assignment that had intrigued her as a student. Fogal's original composition allows the viewer yet another layer of access to the subject through sound.

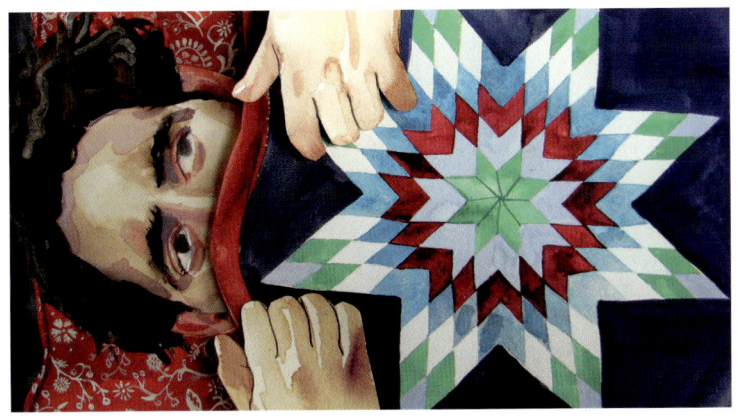

Buffalo Milk Yogurt
By Jennifer Levonian, Philadelphia, Pennsylvania

Digital video/animation, 6:46 minutes, 2010
Collection of the artist

Self-portrait

by Sequoyah Aono

Sequoyah Aono carves self-portraits from wood in what he calls moments of "instability and uncertainty." He considers the act of carving as the force that grounds him, renews his sense of purpose, and gives him roots. Embedded in the surfaces of his wood sculptures is the story of a global artist who was born in Italy, raised in Japan, and recently settled in New York City. Constantly searching to understand what unifies people of diverse backgrounds, he explains, "I feel that humanity is created from the invisible space enveloping each of us and our feelings, such as mercy, love, jealousy and hatred. . . . I try to express this space by carving my own body." The meaning of his self-portraits, therefore, is inseparable from his meditative act of searching for "the reason of existence in this society."

While Aono's approach to his life-size self-portraits is spiritual, drawing on the inspiration he finds in ancient Christian and Buddhist imagery, his technique is physically demanding and rigorous. His process involves first chiseling the figure roughly out of one piece of wood with a chainsaw. He then adds the arms and legs from the discarded wood and carefully carves the details with a chisel, rasp, and file. In order to prevent warps and cracks, he cuts the body in half and hollows out the inside so that the two large pieces of wood are approximately two-and-a-half inches thick. The penultimate step is to reassemble the parts and return the sculpture to an upright position before painting the figure with acrylic. The paint drips over the figure slowly and irregularly, adding texture and emotional resonance to the finished work.

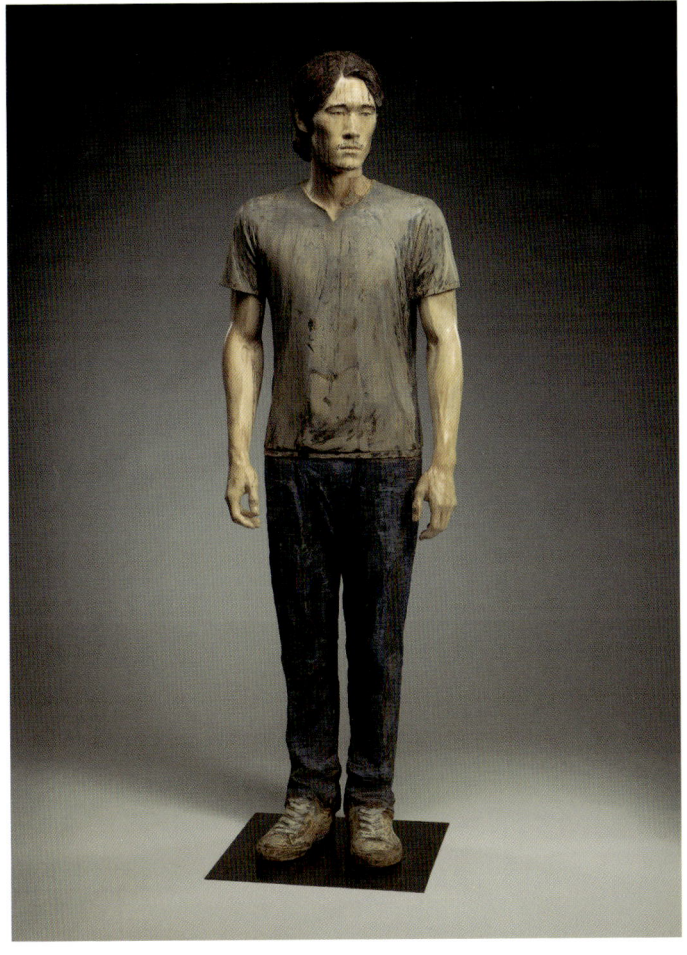

Self-portrait
By Sequoyah Aono, New York City

Acrylic on wood with steel base, 177.8 cm (70 in.) height, 2010
Collection of the artist

COMMENDED

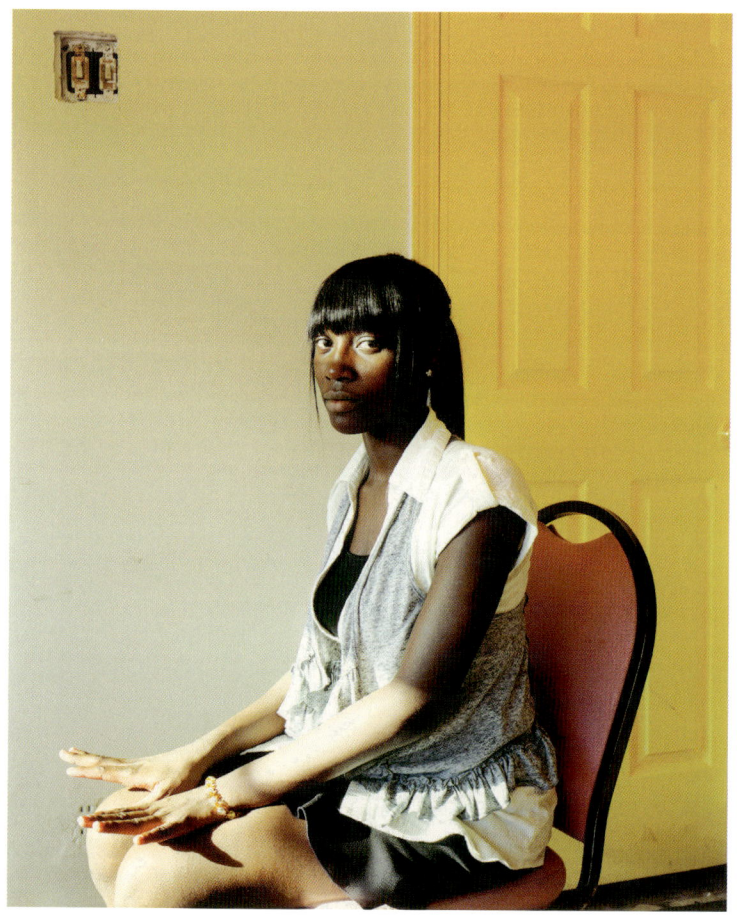

Lillian, New Covenant Church of Deliverance, Chicago, 2011
By Paul D'Amato, Riverside, Illinois

Inkjet print, 101.6 x 76.2 cm (40 x 30 in.), 2011
Collection of the artist, courtesy Stephen Daiter Gallery, Chicago

COMMENDED

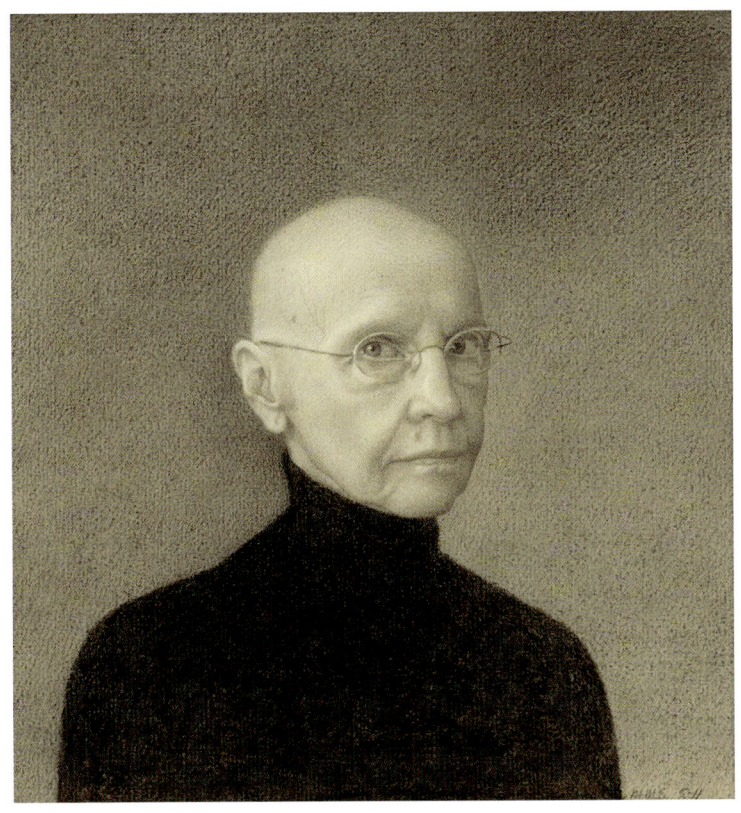

Self-portrait
By Martha Mayer Erlebacher, Elkins Park, Pennsylvania

Nero pencil on paper, 30.5 x 27.9 cm (12 x 11 in.), 2011
Jalane and Richard Davidson

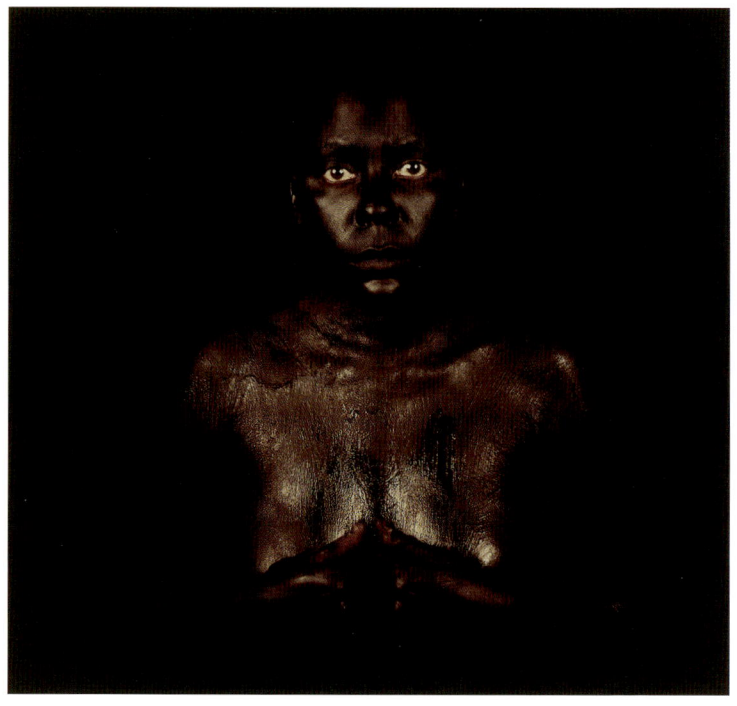

For Delia
By Heidi Fancher, Washington, D.C.

C-print, 87 x 88.9 cm (34¼ x 35 in.) framed, 2010
Collection of the artist

COMMENDED

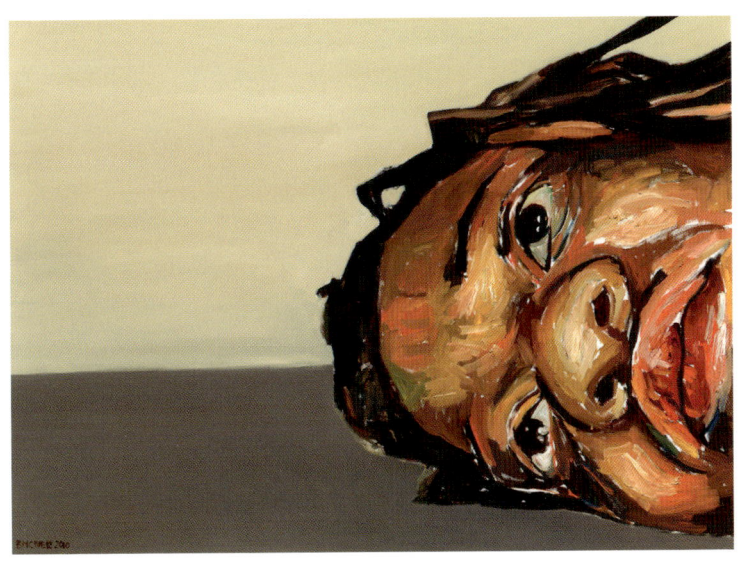

Depression
By Beverly McIver, Durham, North Carolina

Oil on canvas, 91.4 x 121.9 cm (36 x 48 in.), 2010
Collection of the artist, courtesy Betty Cuningham Gallery,
New York City

COMPETITION FINALISTS

(in alphabetical order)

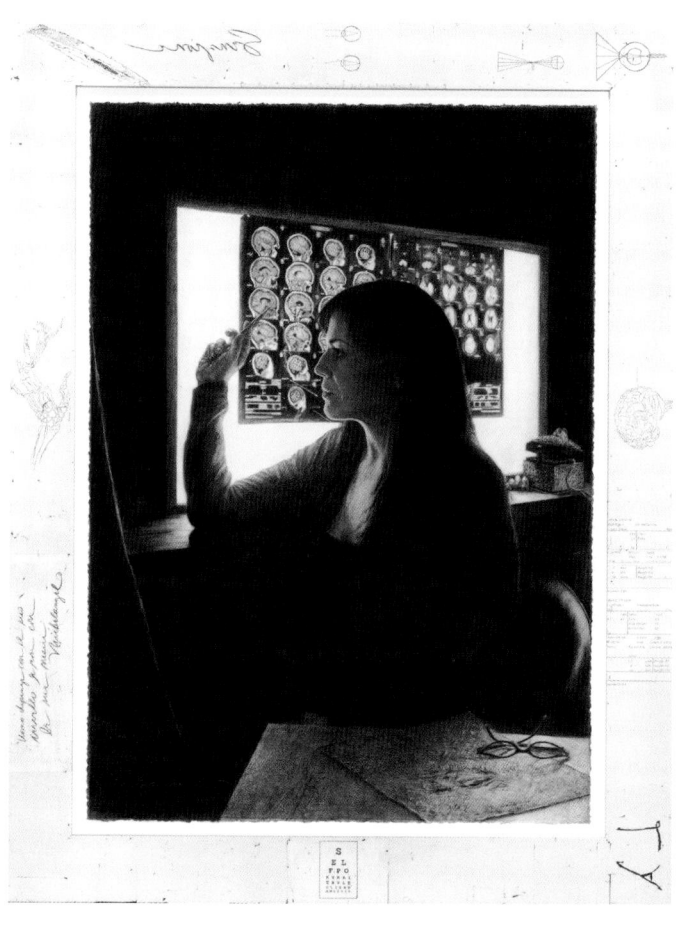

Sensazione: A Self-Portrait
By Leslie Adams, Toledo, Ohio

Charcoal on paper, 107.3 x 75.6 cm (42¼ x 29¾ in.), 2010
Collection of the artist

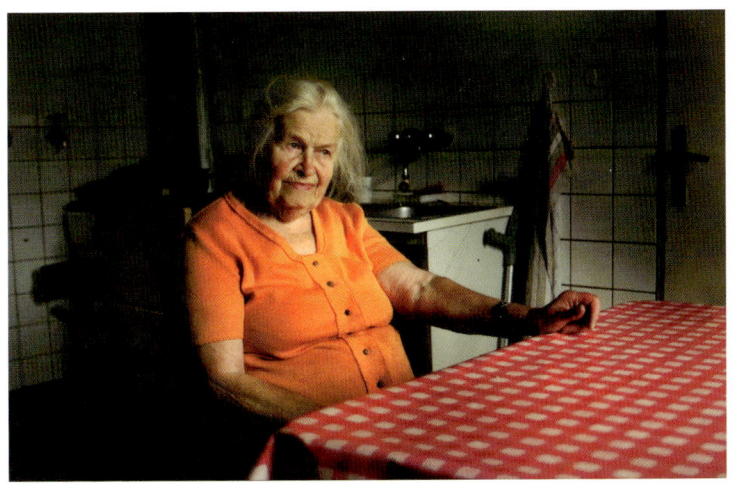

Elisabeth
By Veronika Adaskova, Brooklyn, New York

Archival inkjet print, 29.8 x 44.9 cm (11¾ x 17¹¹/₁₆ in.), 2011
Collection of the artist

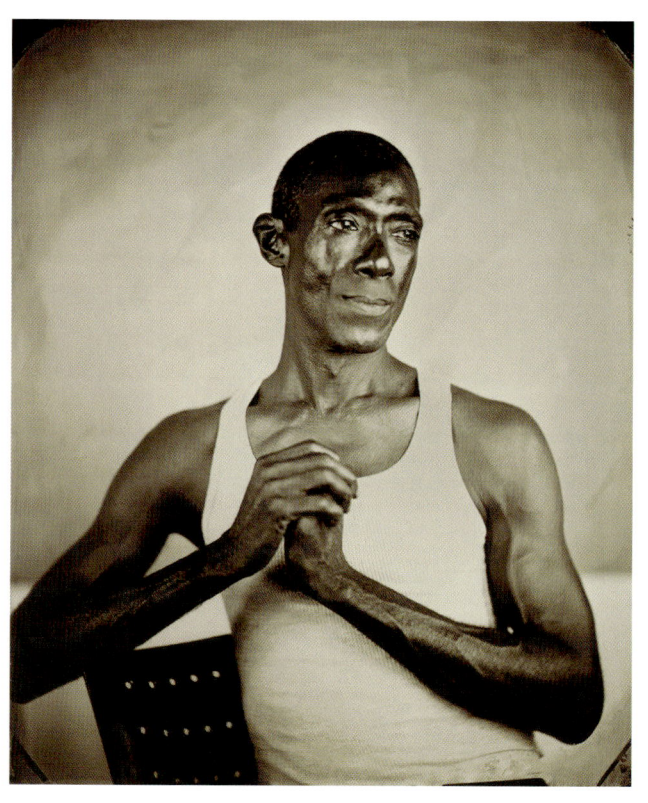

Kevin
By Keliy Anderson-Staley, Russellville, Arkansas

Pigment print from wet-plate collodion tintype photograph,
116.8 x 91.4 cm (46 x 36 in.), 2010
Collection of the artist

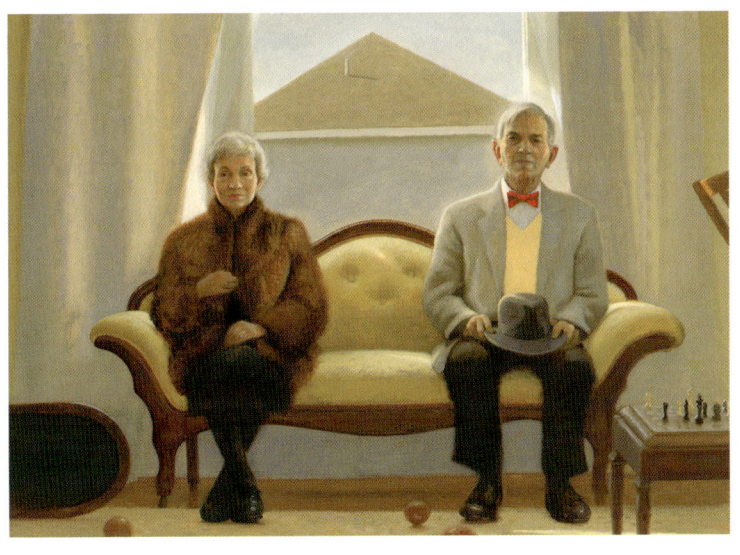

Inheritance
By Bo Bartlett, Vashon, Washington

Oil on linen, 121.9 x 167.6 cm (48 x 66 in.), 2010
Collection of the artist

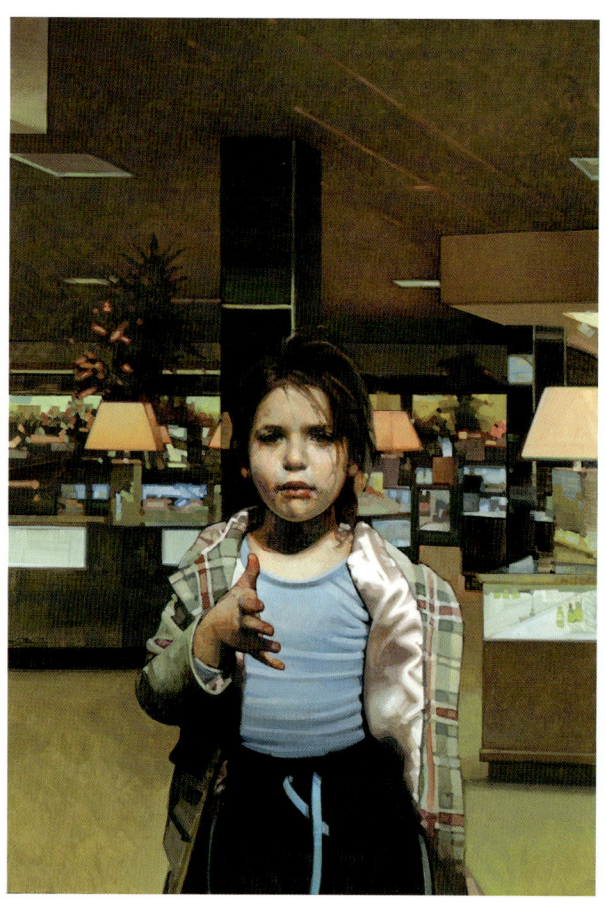

Girl in a Department Store No. 1
By Aaron Morgan Brown, Selinsgrove, Pennsylvania

Oil on panel, 91.4 x 61 cm (36 x 24 in.), 2011
Collection of the artist

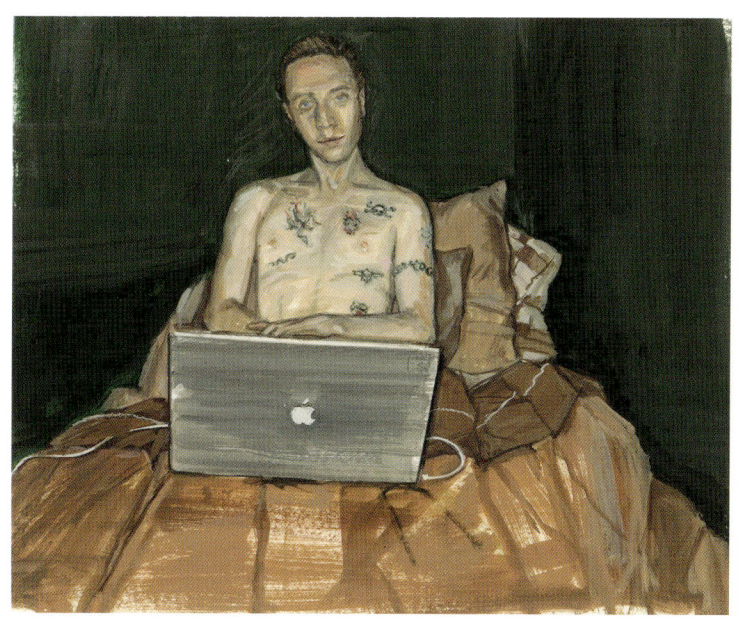

Oliver at 20
By Laura Chasman, Roslindale, Massachusetts

Gouache on museum mounting board, 25.4 x 30.5 cm (10 x 12 in.), 2010
Collection of the artist

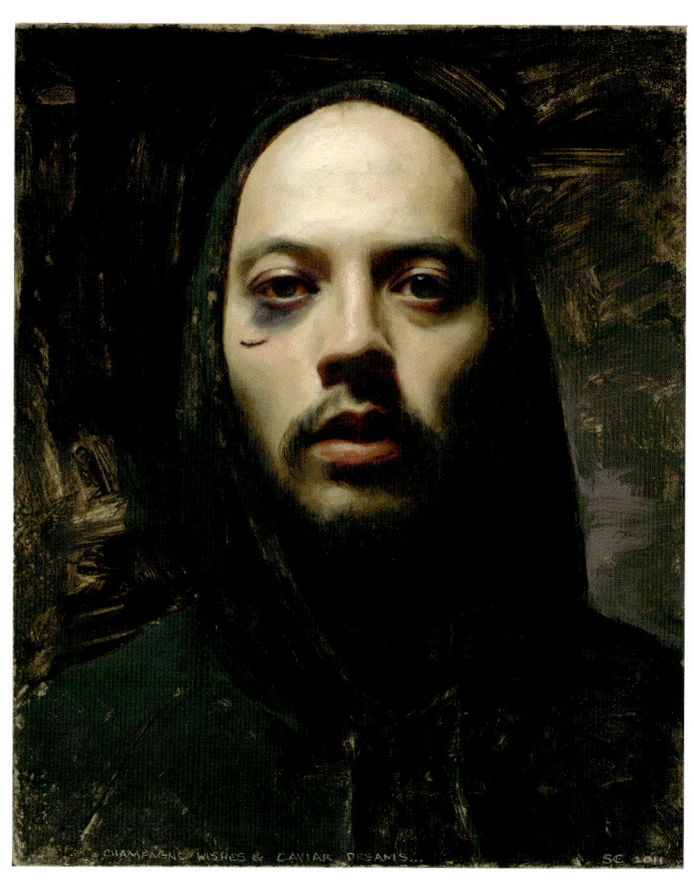

Champagne Wishes and Caviar Dreams . . .
By Sean Cheetham, Los Angeles, California

Oil on prepared paper, 25.4 x 20.3 cm (10 x 8 in.), 2011
Jay Bentley and Natalia Fabia

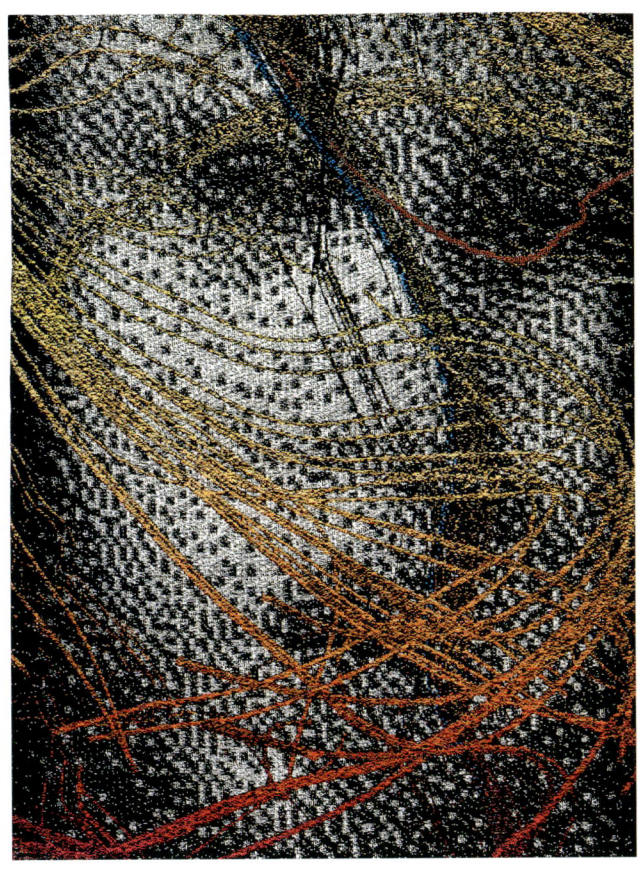

Su Brain Tracts
By Lia Cook, Berkeley, California

Hand-woven cotton and rayon, 170.2 x 127 cm (67 x 50 in.), 2011
Collection of the artist

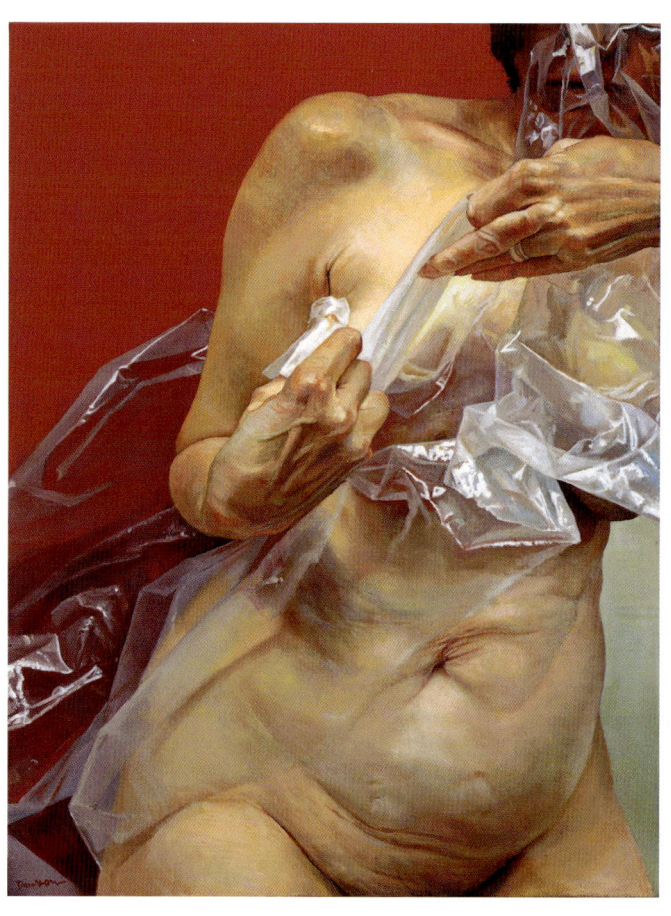

Modesty2
By Lynn Davison, Naples, Florida

Oil on canvas, 81.9 x 60.6 cm (32¼ x 23⅞ in.), 2010
Collection of the artist

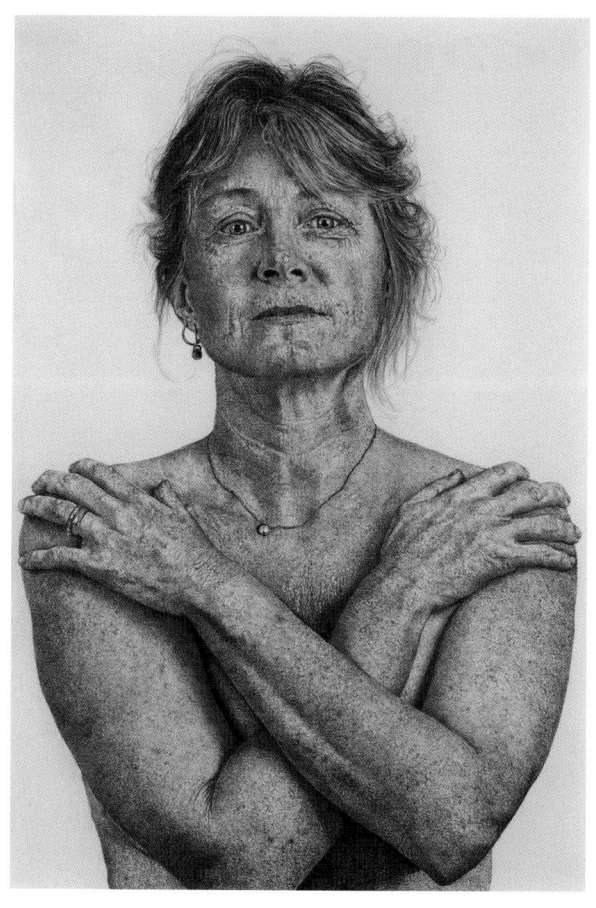

Marie
By Ray DiCapua, Storrs, Connecticut

Charcoal on paper, 190.5 x 124.5 cm (75 x 49 in.), 2011
Collection of the artist

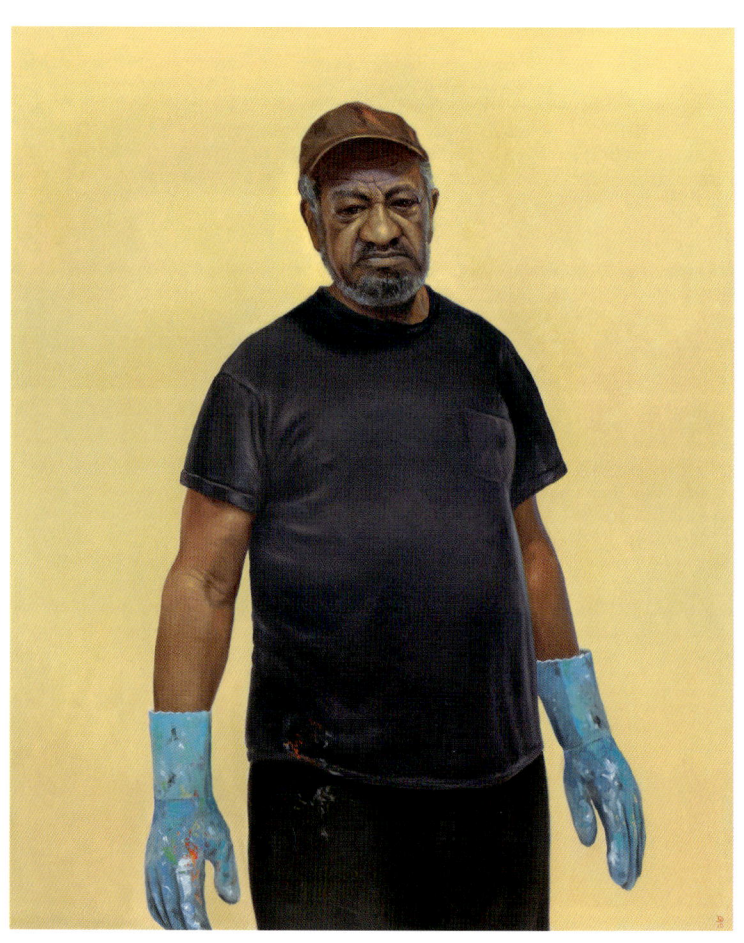

Mike
By Willard Dixon, San Rafael, California

Oil on canvas, 152.4 x 121.9 cm (60 x 48 in.), 2010
Collection of the artist

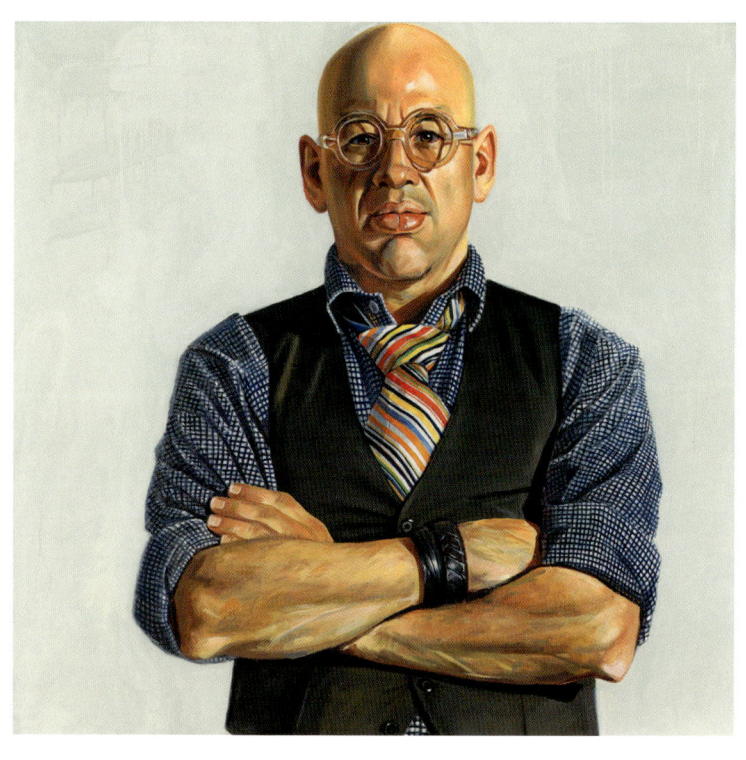

Room and Board
By Tim Doud, Washington, D.C.

Oil on linen, 101.6 x 101.6 cm (40 x 40 in.), 2010
Collection of the artist

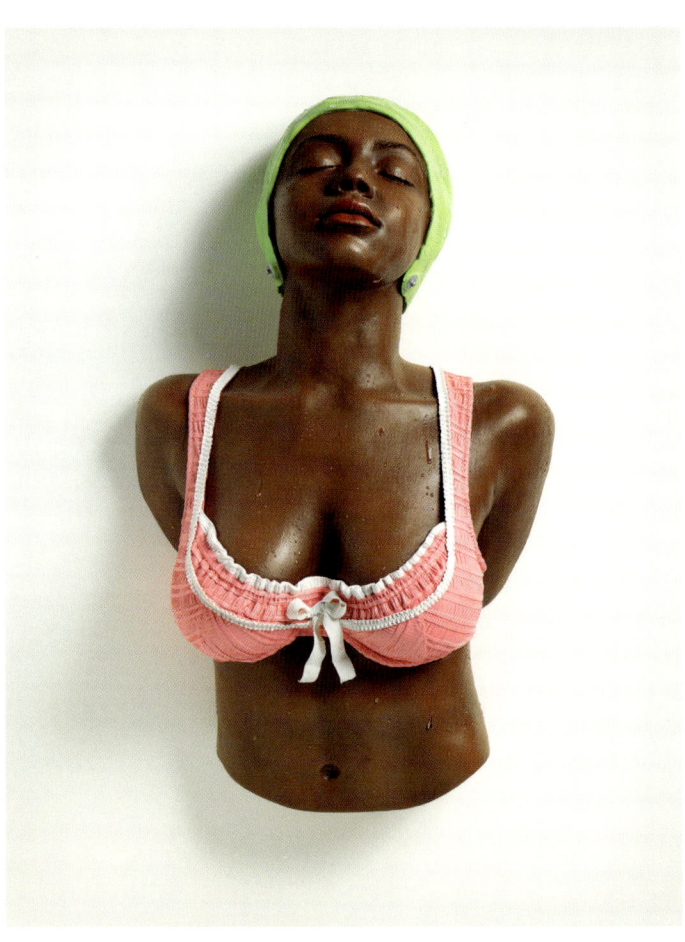

General's Daughter
By Carole Feuerman, New York City

Oil on resin, 61 cm (24 in.) height, 2011
Collection of the artist, courtesy of Jim Kempner Fine Art, New York City

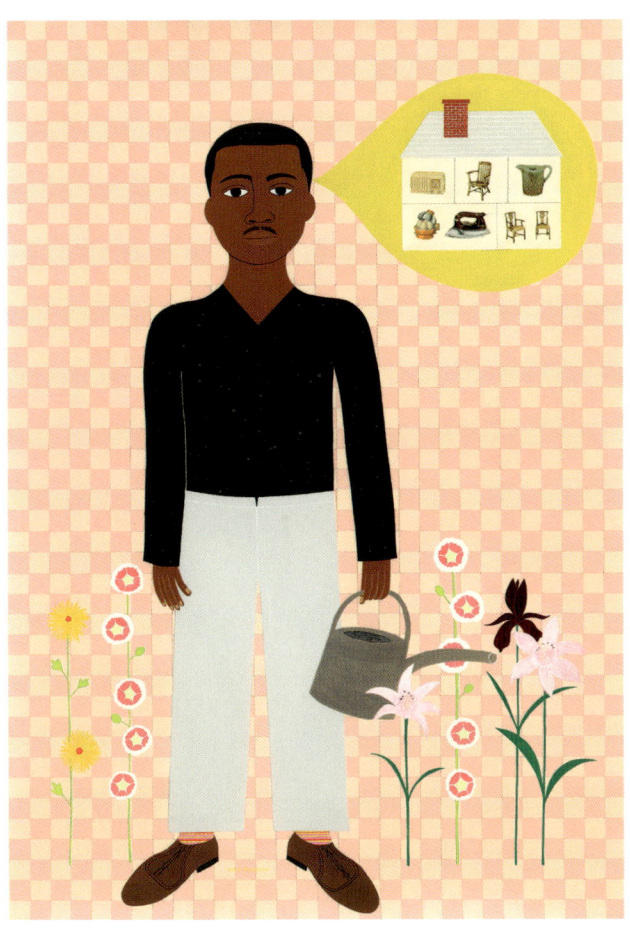

Arthur Waters the Garden
By Lucy Fradkin, Staten Island, New York

Mixed media, 112.1 x 76.2 cm (44$\frac{1}{8}$ x 30 in.), 2011
Collection of the artist

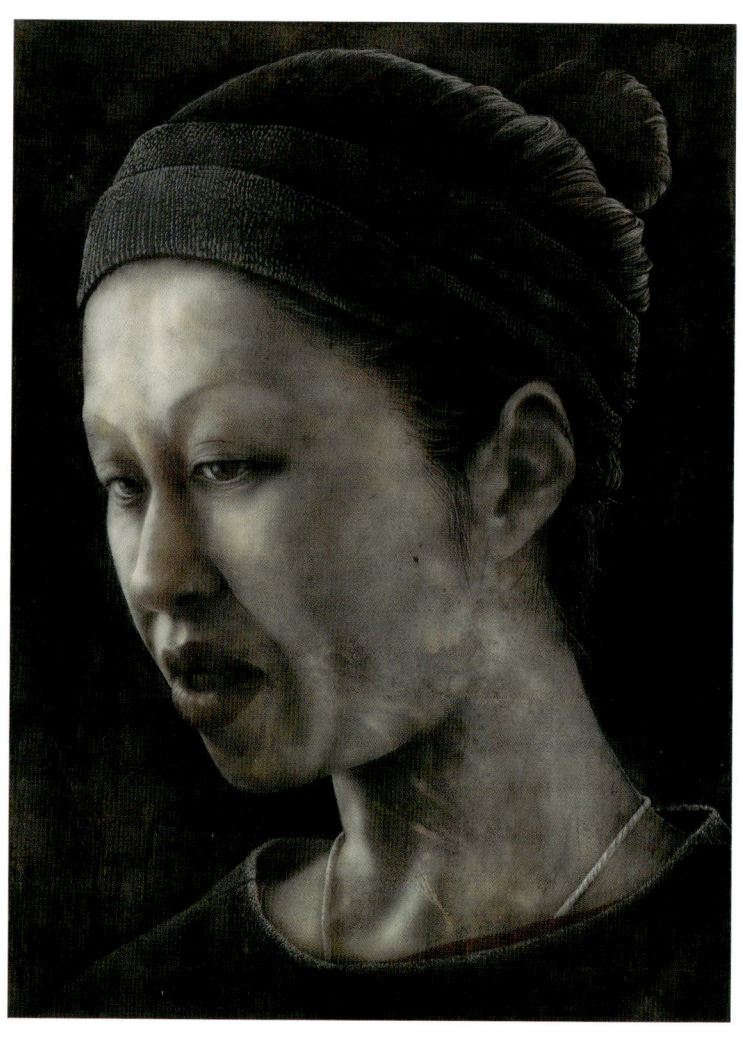

Aki
By Rieko Fujinami, Beacon, New York

Mixed media on acrylic mirror, 121.9 x 87.6 cm (48 x 34½ in.), 2011
Collection of the artist

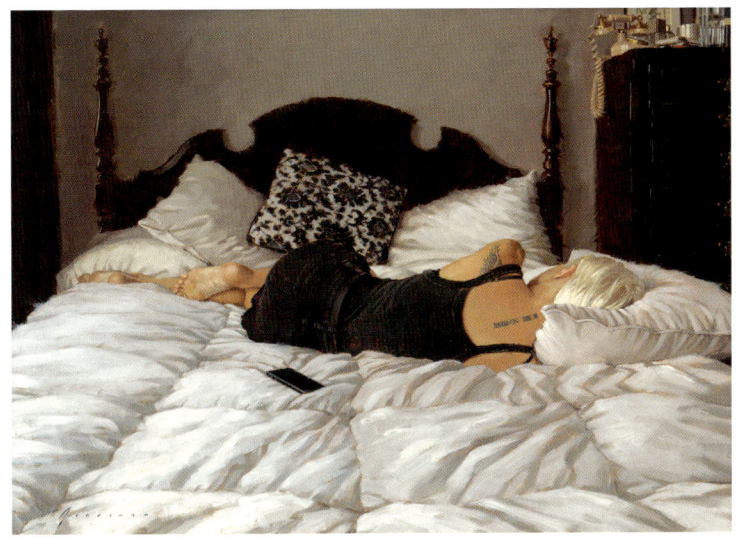

City Girl
By Vincent Giarrano, Washington Depot, Connecticut

Oil on board, 45.7 x 61 cm (18 x 24 in.), 2011
Collection of the artist

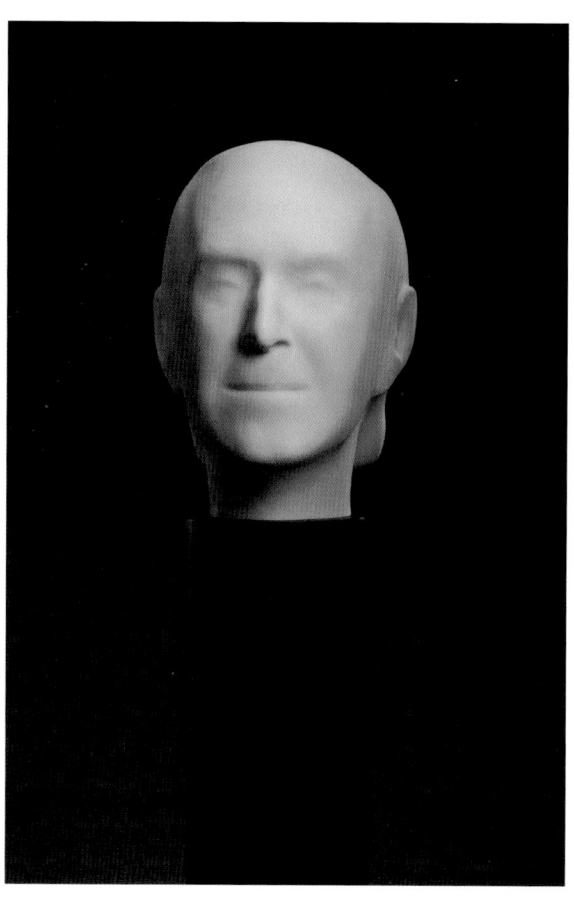

César Pelli
By Philip Grausman, Washington, Connecticut

Plaster, 170.8 cm (67¼ in.) height including base, 2011
Collection of the artist

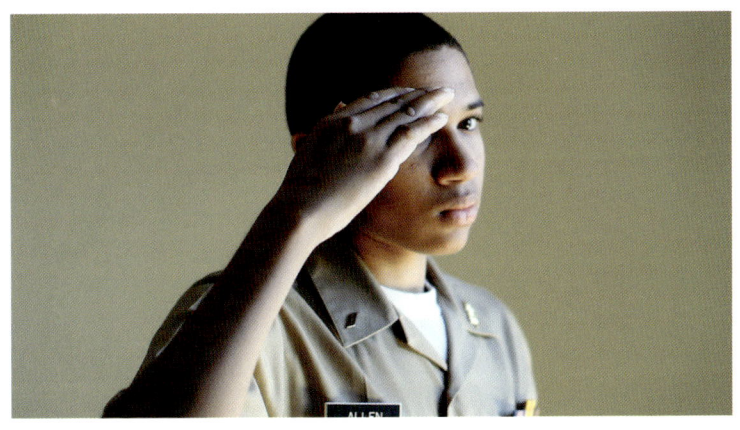

Sharrod (Turn/Twirl)
By Jason Hanasik, San Francisco, California

HD video, infinite loop, 2011
Collection of the artist

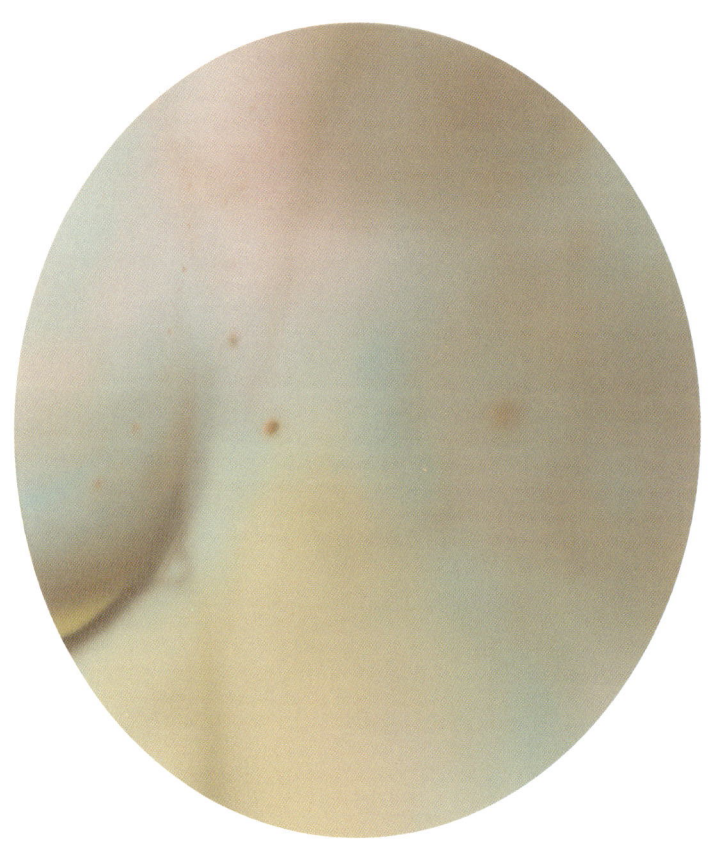

Body 10/17/11
By Gwen Hardie, New York City

Oil on canvas, 91.4 x 76.2 cm (36 x 30 in.), 2011
Collection of the artist

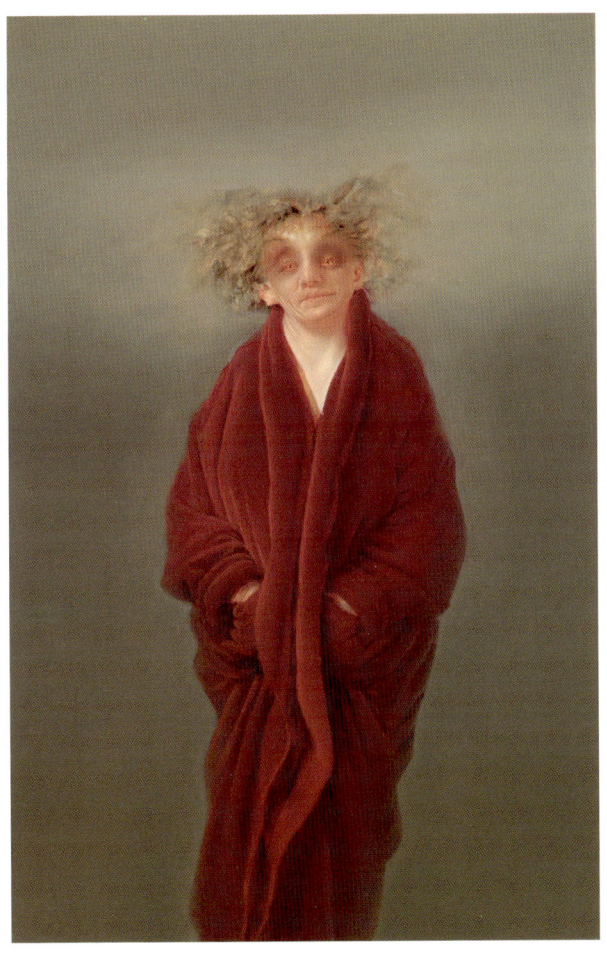

Portrait (Red Robe)
By Anne Harris, Riverside, Illinois

Oil on linen, 132.1 x 83.8 cm (52 x 33 in.), 2008–12
Collection of the artist, courtesy of Alexandre Gallery, New York City

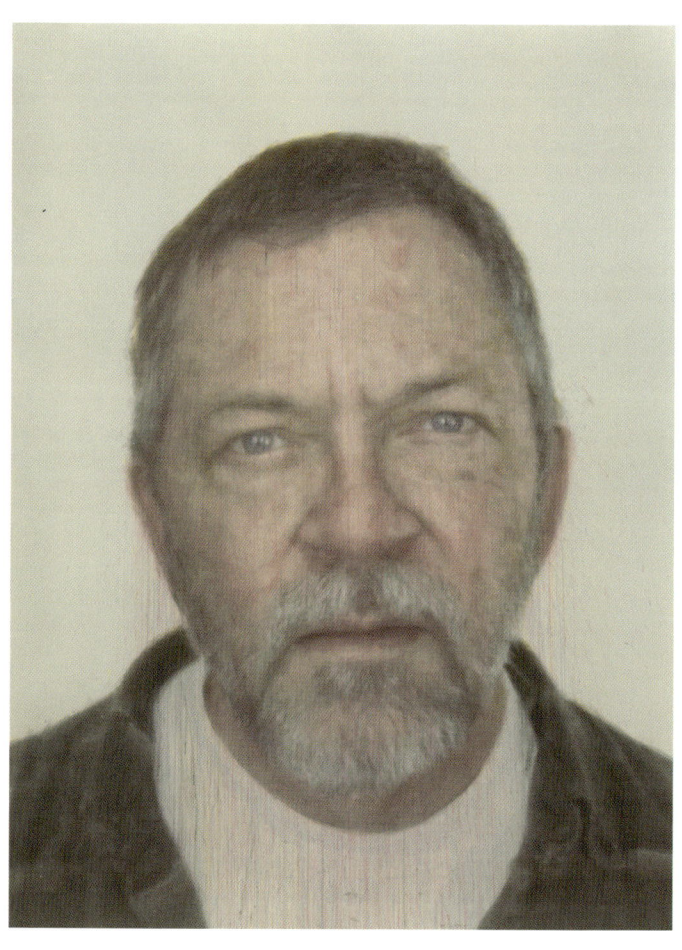

John H.
By Erik Hougen, Brooklyn, New York

Watercolor on paper, 203.2 x 144.8 cm (80 x 57 in.), 2010
Collection of the artist

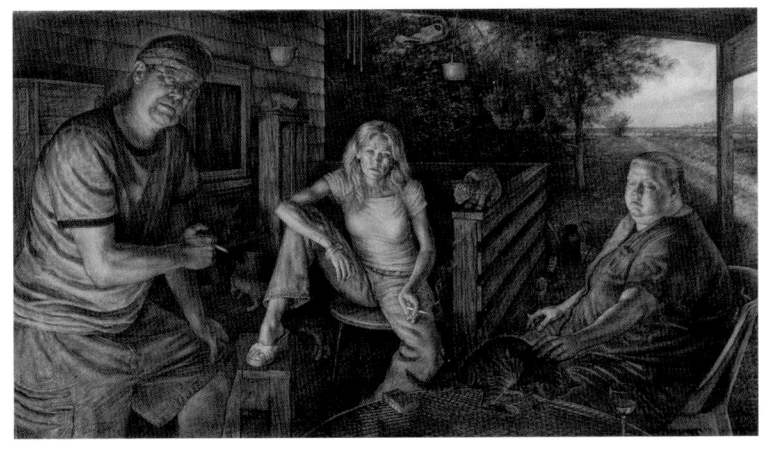

David and Anita Visiting Daina
By Edgar Jerins, New York City

Charcoal on paper, 142.2 x 243.8 cm (56 x 96 in.), 2011
Collection of the artist, courtesy ACA Galleries, New York City

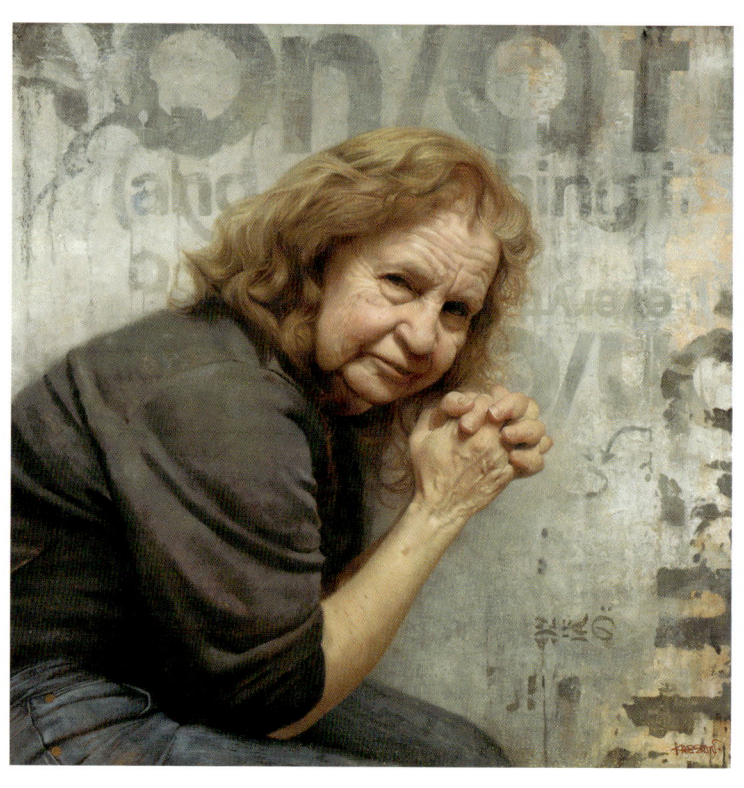

Portrait of My Mom, Roberta
By David Kassan, Brooklyn, New York

Oil on panel, 63.5 x 61 cm (25 x 24 in.), 2010
Collection of Robin and Michael Wilkinson

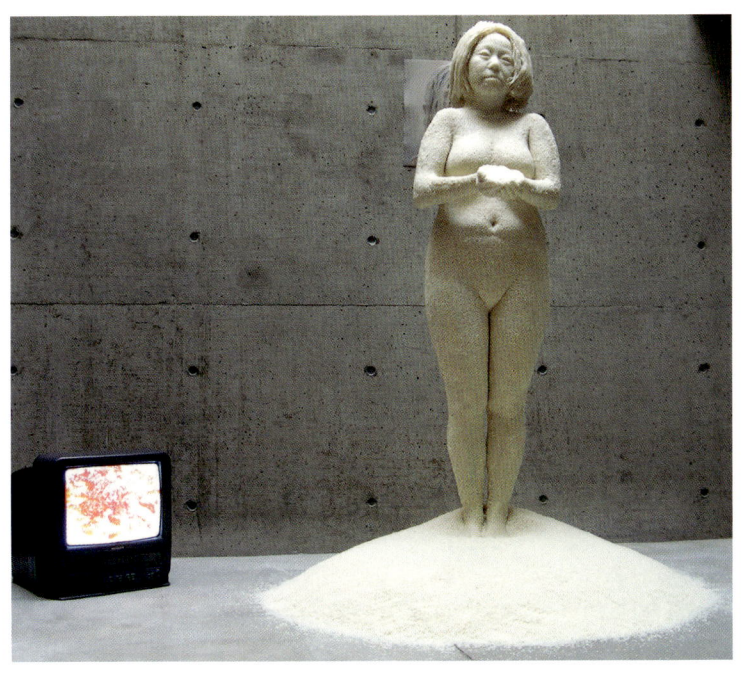

100 Pounds of Rice
By Saeri Kiritani, Forest Hills, New York

Rice, rice noodles, Elmer's Glue, epoxy glue, wood, and metal sticks,
165.1 cm (65 in.) height, including base, 2010
Collection of the artist

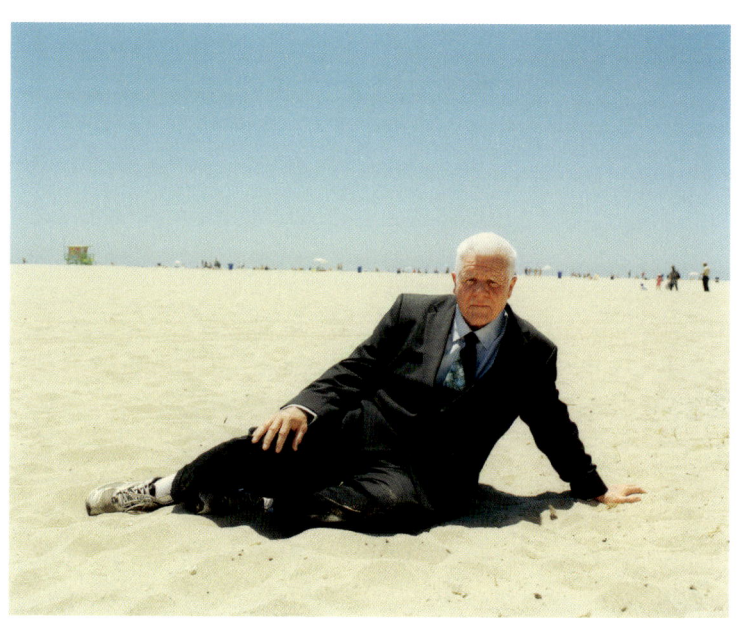

Uncle Fred in Santa Monica
By Bridget Lanigan, Coram, New York

Digital C-print, 61 x 71.1 cm (24 x 28 in.), 2010
Collection of the artist

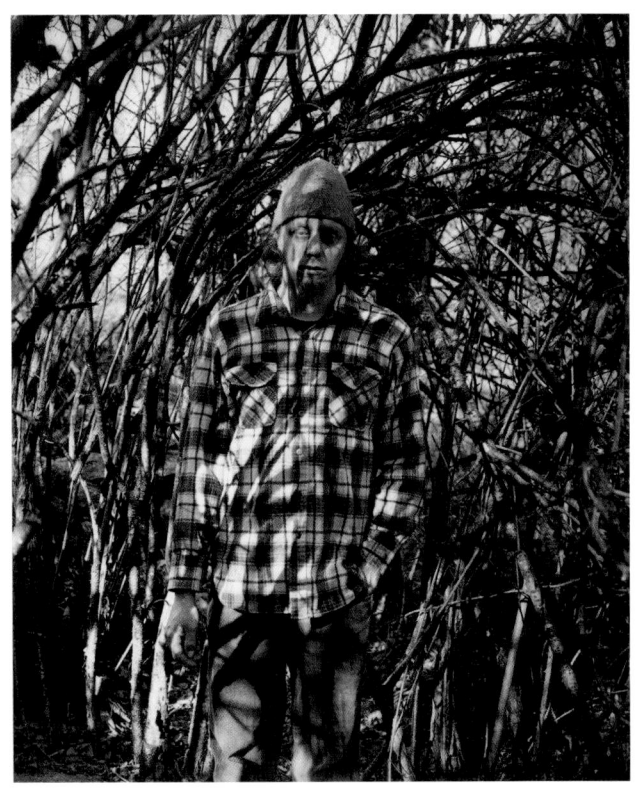

Untitled, from the *Loveland Series*
By Megan Ledbetter, Jamaica Plain, Massachusetts

Gelatin silver print, 57.2 x 45.7 cm (22½ x 18 in.), 2010
Collection of the artist

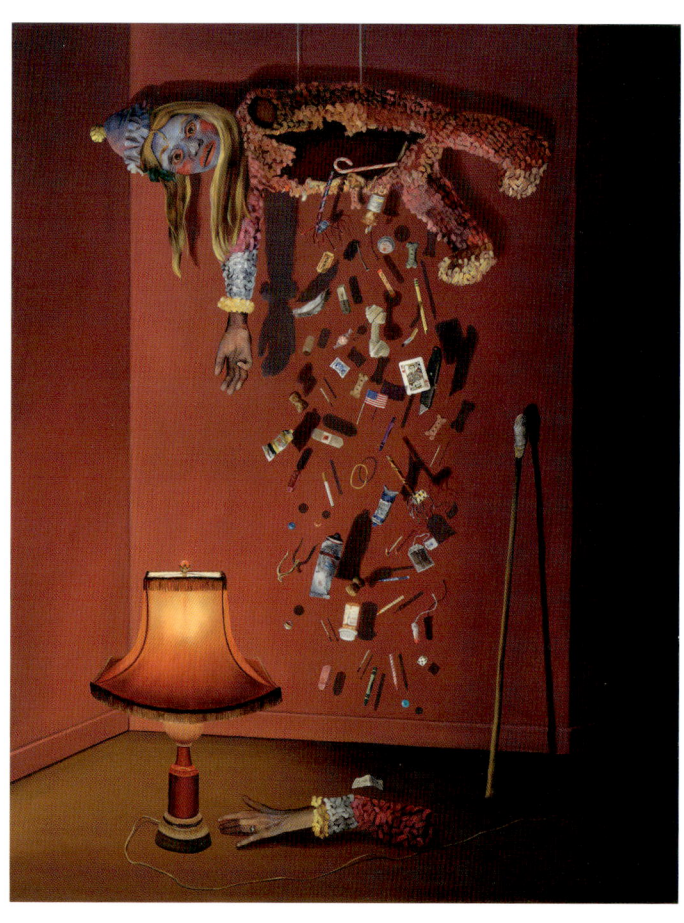

Piñata
By Tina Mion, Winslow, Arizona

Oil on linen, 213.4 x 162.6 cm (84 x 64 in), 2010
Collection of the artist

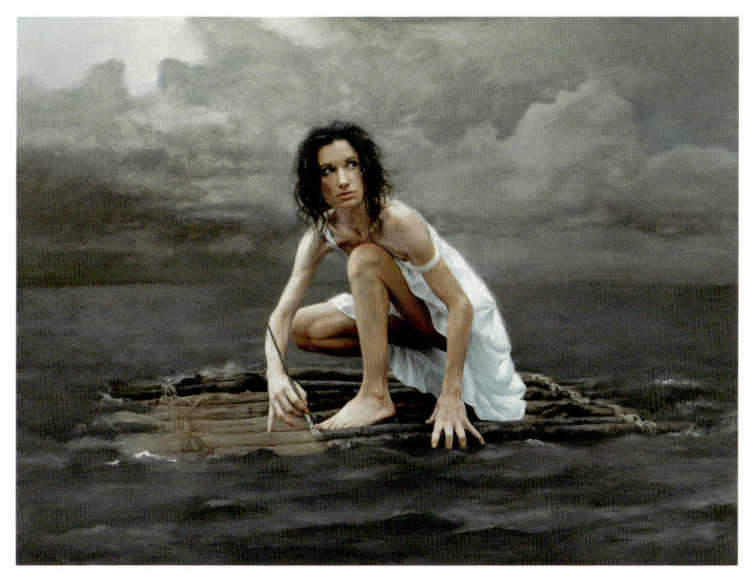

Life Raft
By Katie O'Hagan, Beacon, New York

Oil on canvas, 116 x 152.4 cm (46 x 60 in.), 2011
Collection of the artist

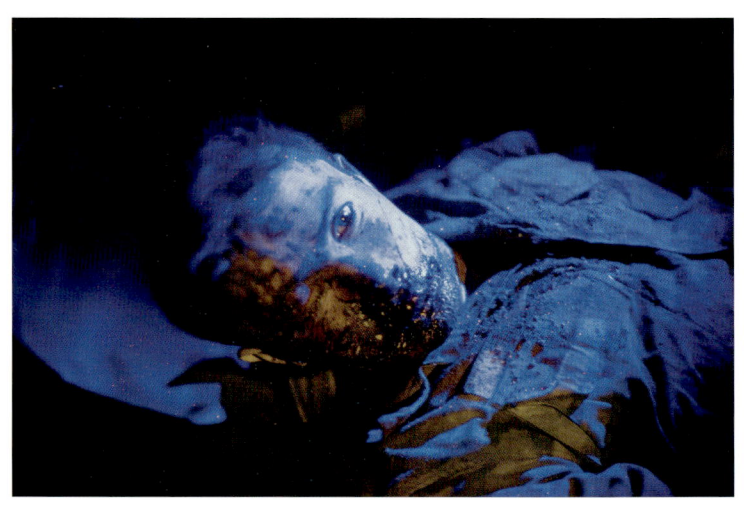

Night Raid
By Louie Palu, Washington, D.C.

Pigment print, 50.8 x 61 cm (20 x 24 in.), 2010
Collection of the artist

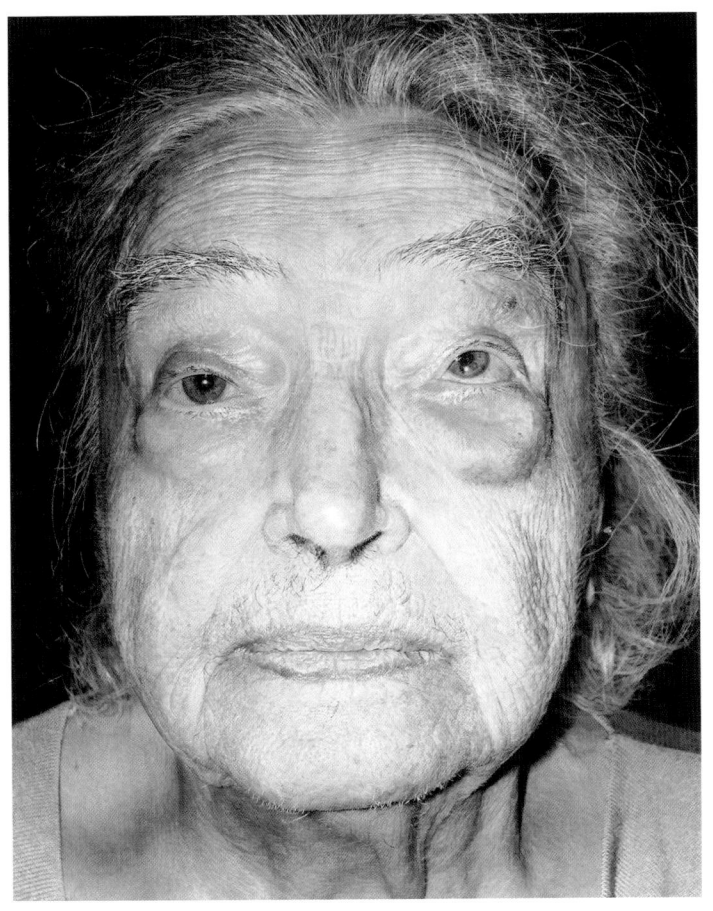

Maryanna
By Bly Pope, New Richmond, Wisconsin

Graphite and ink on illustration board, 99.7 x 77.5 cm
(39¼ x 30½ in.), 2011
Collection of the artist

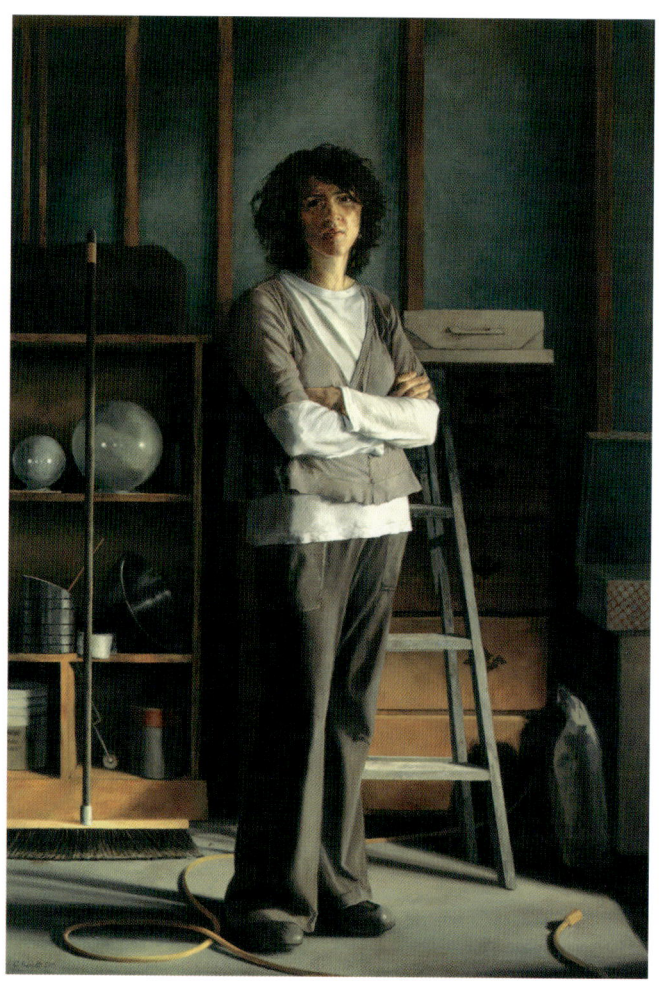

Legacy: Portrait of Val
By Catherine Prescott, Mechanicsburg, Pennsylvania

Oil on canvas, 182.9 x 121.9 cm (72 x 48 in.), 2010
Collection of the artist

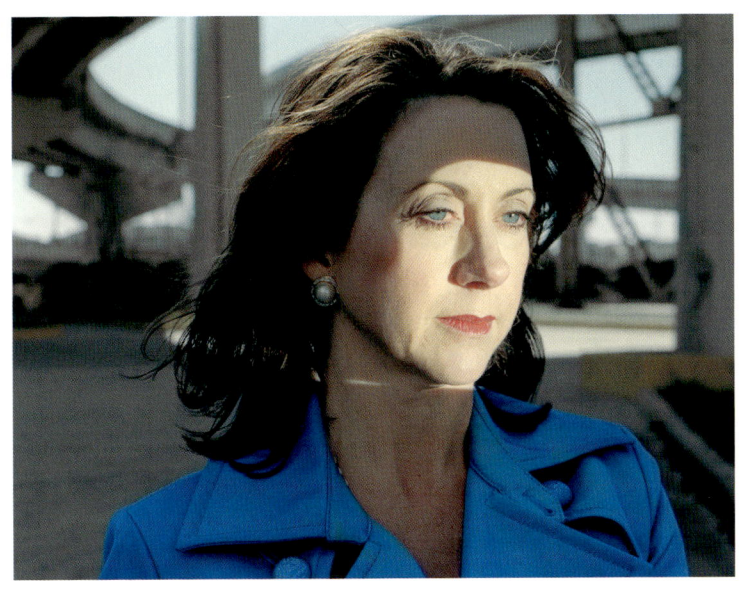

Leslie
By Caitlin Teal Price, Washington, D.C.

Archival pigment print, 73.7 x 91.4 cm (29 x 36 in.), 2010
Collection of the artist

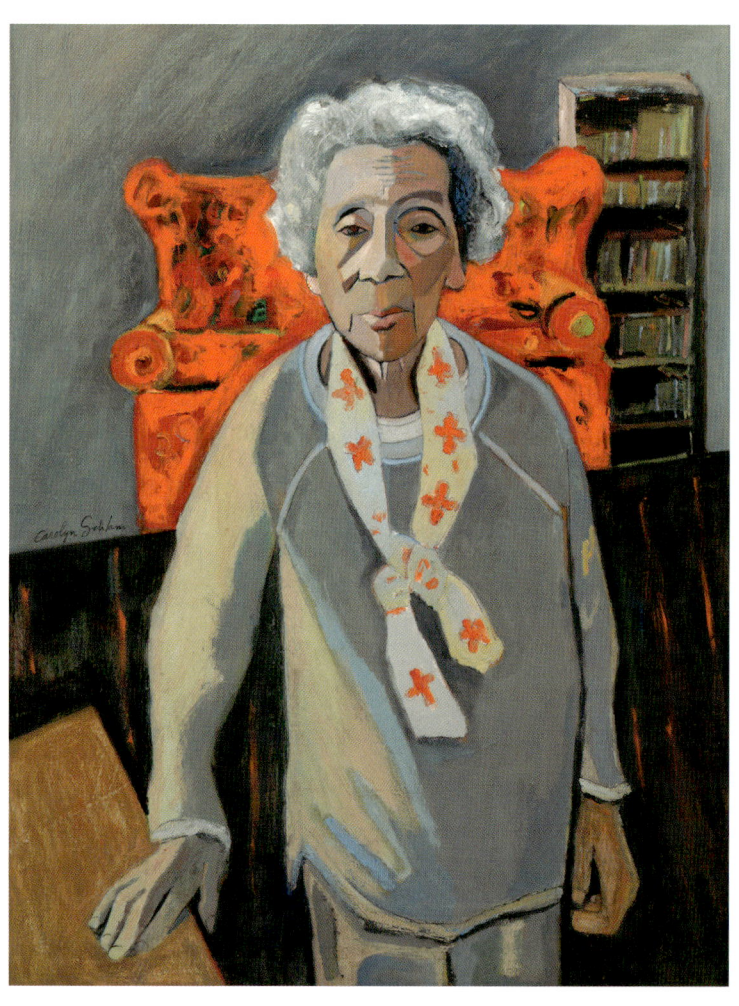

Frances at 103
By Carolyn Schlam, Taos, New Mexico

Oil on canvas, 101.6 x 76.2 cm (40 x 30 in.), 2011
Collection of the artist

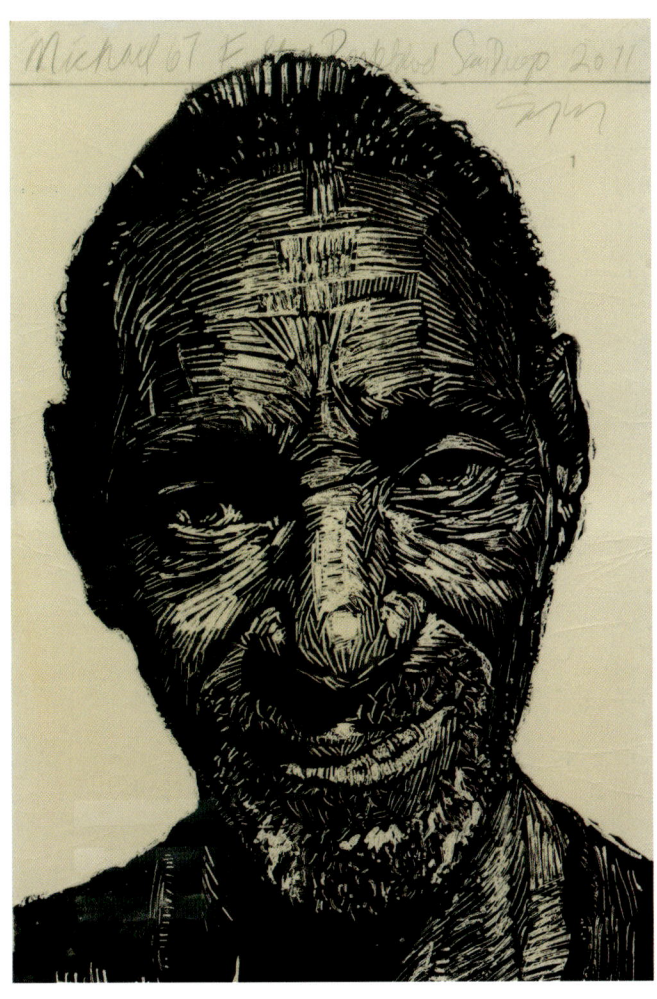

Michael 67 (Pastor Shelby)
By Neil Shigley, San Diego, California

Plexiglas-block print on paper, mounted on canvas, 182.9 x 121.9 cm
(72 x 48 in.), 2011
Collection of the artist

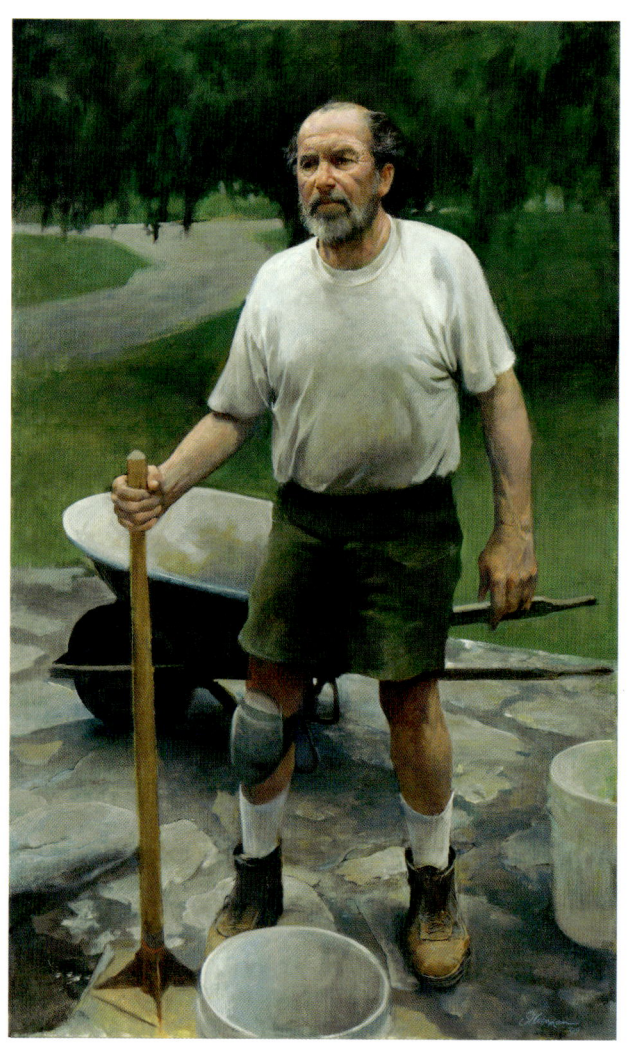

Stonemason
By Burton Philip Silverman, New York City

Oil on linen, 127 x 76.2 cm (50 x 30 in.), 2010
Collection of the artist

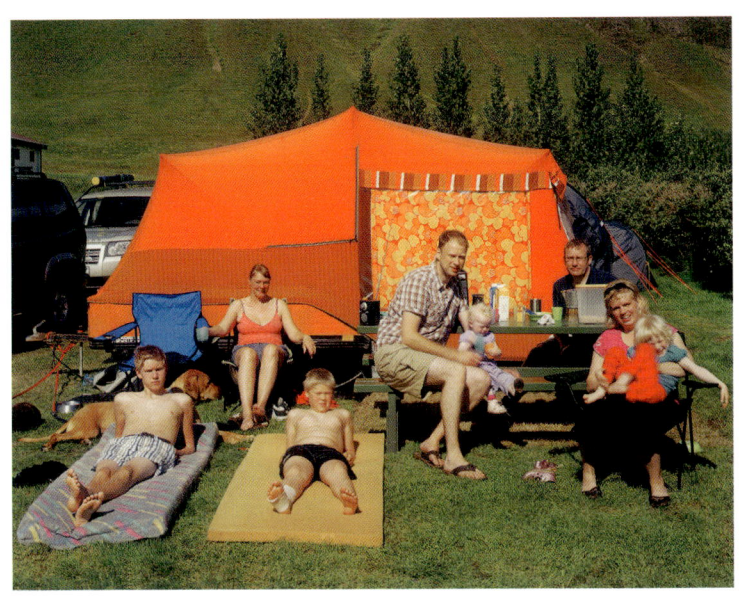

Two Families at Kirkjubaejarklaustur, Iceland
By Michael A. Smith, Ottsville, Pennsylvania

Archival inkjet print, 111.8 x 139.7 cm (44 x 55 in.), 2010
Collection of the artist

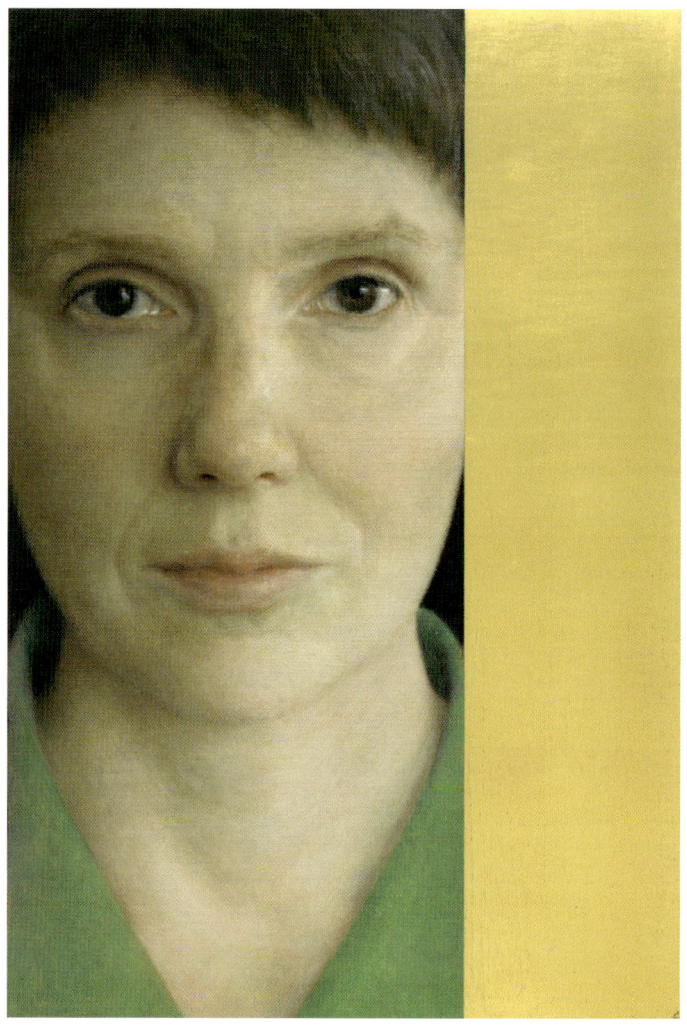

The Birth of Inez Imake
By Ginny Stanford, Sebastopol, California

Acrylic and gold leaf on linen and wood panel, 30.5 x 21 cm
(12 x 8¼ in.), 2011
Collection of the artist

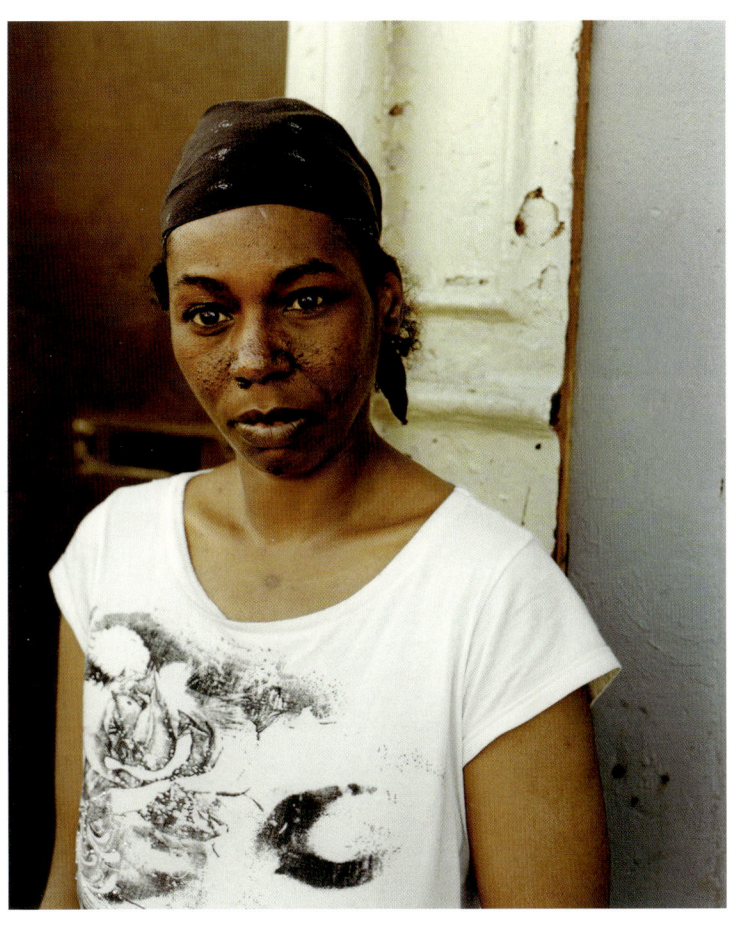

Cathy, Market Street, Paterson, NJ
By Tema Stauffer, Brooklyn, New York

Digital C-print, 76.2 x 61 cm (30 x 24 in.), 2011
Collection of the artist

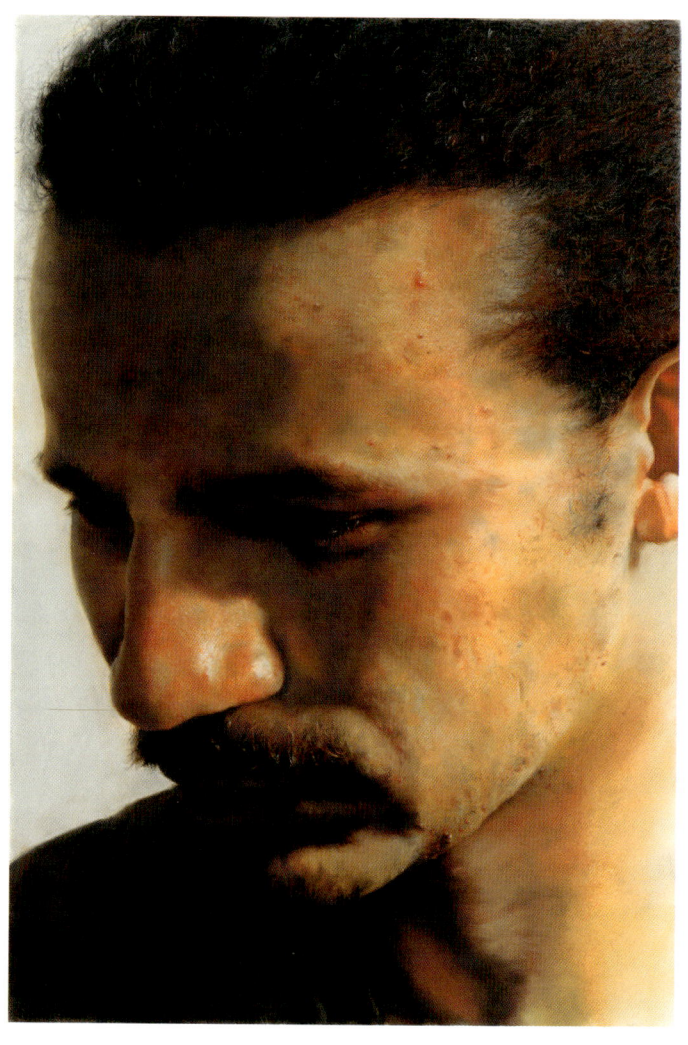

Undefined #2
By Tun Ping Wang, Long Island City, New York

Pastel on paper, 152.4 x 101.6 cm (60 x 40 in.), 2011
Collection of the artist

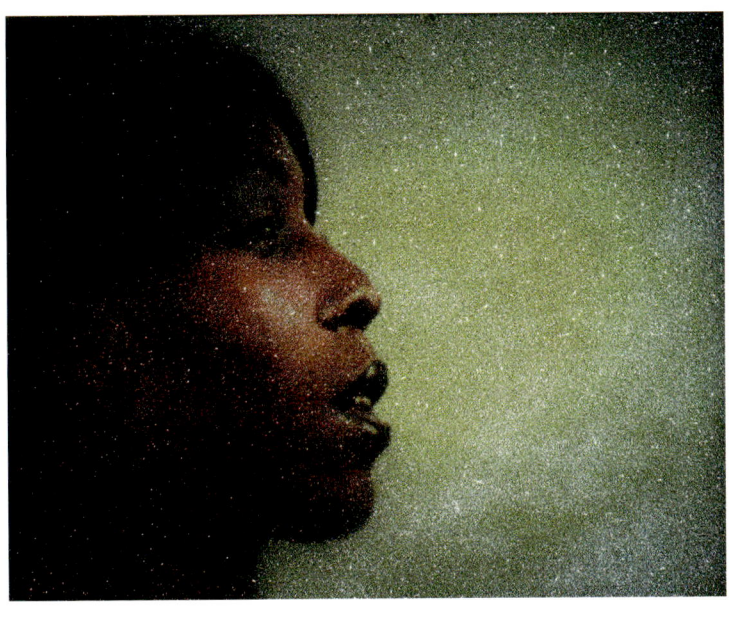

The Gilding of Lily
By Jill Wissmiller, Memphis, Tennessee

Video projected on glitter screen, 2:50 minutes; screen, 152.4 x 203.2 cm
(60 x 80 in.), 2011
Collection of the artist

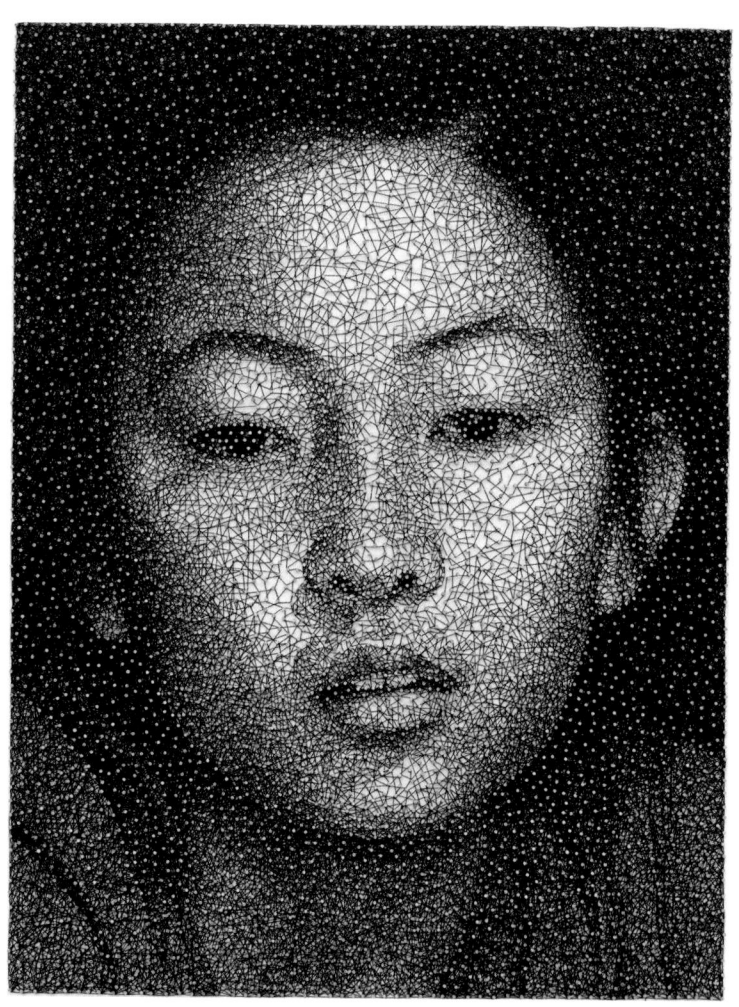

Constellation—Mana
By Kumi Yamashita, New York City

Brads and single, unbroken thread on wood panel, 40.6 x 30.5 cm
(16 x 12 in.), 2011
Collection of the artist

ACKNOWLEDGMENTS

Dorothy Moss, Assistant Curator of Painting and Sculpture, and Director, Outwin Boochever Portrait Competition 2013

This exhibition is truly a collaborative project. The National Portrait Gallery staff and many colleagues beyond the Gallery's walls contributed immeasurably to the success of the third Outwin Boochever Portrait Competition, and we are deeply grateful to them. Our profound thanks go first and foremost to the late Virginia Outwin Boochever, whose creative vision is realized in this exhibition and whose generous spirit continues to inspire American artists' diverse approaches to portraiture through the competition that she endowed. We are enormously grateful for the support of her children, David, Emily, John, and Mary Boochever, and their spouses, Kathleen, William Dana, Carol, and Kevin Teare. Their dedication, insight, and enthusiasm have allowed the competition to attain the dynamism it has today.

Preparing for the selection of finalists and prizewinners involves the entire Portrait Gallery staff. Special thanks go to colleagues in the curatorial departments, who carefully reviewed the initial entries: Brandon Brame Fortune, Anne Collins Goodyear, Frank H. Goodyear III, Wendy Wick Reaves, and Ann Shumard. Wendy, currently also serving as interim director, and Brandon, who is chief curator, also served on the jury, and their expertise in the selection process was invaluable. Brandon deserves particular recognition for launching this program in 2005. I am honored to be continuing her superb work on the competition and grateful to her for entrusting me with its direction.

We would also like to thank Nik Apostolides, associate director; Claire Kelly, Kristin Smith, and Beth Isaacson of the Office of Exhibitions; John McMahon, Todd Gardner, Molly Grimsley, Dale Hunt, Wayne Long, and Jennifer Wodzianski in the Office of the Registrar; Dru Dowdy, director of publications; Tibor

Waldner, Michael Baltzer, Alex Cooper, Raymond Cunningham, Nekisha Durrett, Grant Lazer, Saul Moss, Christy Thorley, and Caroline Wooden in the Office of Design and Production; Deb Sisum and Benjamin Bloom in the Office of New Media; photographer Mark Gulezian; conservators Lou Molnar and Rosemary Fallon; Rebecca Kasemeyer, Ian Cooke, and Geri Provost Lyons in the Office of Education; writer/researcher Warren Perry; Bethany Bentley, public affairs specialist; Rich Reichley in the Office of Administration and Operations; Kristy Snaman in the Office of External Affairs; and Liz Johnson, curatorial assistant. Heartfelt thanks go to former curatorial assistant Lauren Johnson, whose preparatory work on the competition allowed the process to go smoothly even after she left NPG for graduate school. Laura Revello worked diligently on the competition during the call for entries, managed the online submissions, and graciously returned to assist with both jury meetings. Intern Hillary-Morgan Watt helped with the first jury meeting in the spring of 2012. My deepest thanks go to intern Lizzie Stein, whose professionalism and attention to detail ensured that we produced an exhibition worthy of the high quality of the finalists' work.

The Outwin Boochever Portrait Competition 2013 reached the public first through the work of our colleagues at CallForEntry.org, a service of WESTAF. We are grateful to Raquel Vasquez of WESTAF for working with us to ensure that the entry process went smoothly. The staff at ARTEX Fine Art Services, including John Jacobs, Kit Lee, Heidi Elliott, Ting Siu Ip, Wayne Boone, Orville Walker, Mark Haynes, Bob Ikena, and Graham Childs, provided both a wonderful space, conducive to meaningful discussion for our final jury day, and expert assistance with the shipping, unpacking, and storage of the semifinalists' work. Our deep appreciation goes to Rosemary DeRosa, who once again managed a million details for picking up, returning, and caring for the objects. Debra Naylor at Naylor Design created a dynamic look for the 2013 competition and produced this handsome catalogue.

Our external jurors—Peter Frank, Hung Liu, Richard Powell, and Alec Soth—deserve high praise for their commitment to the artists who entered and for their careful selection of the exhibition. We are indebted to them for being intensely critical and thoughtful in choosing the finalists and prizewinners. We also owe enormous thanks to Mary Sheriff, W. R. Kenan, Jr., Distinguished Professor of Art History at the University of North Carolina, Chapel Hill, for linking historical work and contemporary portraiture in a provocative, illuminating essay.

This competition would not be what it is without the artists' commitment to portraiture. More than 3,000 artists living and working in the United States took the time to answer the call for entries, and we are grateful to each of them for their interest in the National Portrait Gallery. We are always pleased to see artists from former competitions reentering their work, and we encourage those who were not chosen this time to submit work again in the future since our jury changes with each competition. Because of the dedication of everyone mentioned here, the bar has been set high; we await the 2016 competition with great expectations.

INDEX OF ARTISTS

Italicized page numbers refer to illustrations.